Guided Inquiry Design

Recent Titles in the
Libraries Unlimited Guided Inquiry Series

Seeking Meaning: A Process Approach to Library and Information Services, Second Edition
Carol C. Kuhlthau

Guided Inquiry: Learning in the 21st Century
Carol C. Kuhlthau, Leslie K. Maniotes, and Ann K. Caspari

Guided Inquiry Design

A Framework for Inquiry in Your School

Carol C. Kuhlthau,
Leslie K. Maniotes, and
Ann K. Caspari

Libraries Unlimited Guided Inquiry Series

LIBRARIES UNLIMITED

AN IMPRINT OF ABC-CLIO, LLC
Santa Barbara, California • Denver, Colorado • Oxford, England

Library of Congress Cataloging-in-Publication Data

Kuhlthau, Carol Collier, 1937– author.
  Guided inquiry design : a framework for inquiry in your school / Carol C. Kuhlthau, Leslie K. Maniotes, and Ann K. Caspari.
        pages cm. — (Libraries Unlimited guided inquiry series)
  Includes bibliographical references and index.
    ISBN 978-1-61069-009-6 (paperback : alk. paper) — ISBN 978-1-61069-010-2 (ebook)
  1. Learning.   2. Motivation in education.   3. Information literacy—Study and teaching (Higher)
4. Information technology.   I. Maniotes, Leslie K., 1967– author.   II. Caspari, Ann K., 1965– author.
III. Title.
  LB1060.K83   2012
  370.15'4—dc23   2012014492

ISBN: 978-1-61069-009-6
EISBN: 978-1-61069-010-2

23 22 21 20 19 18 17   8 9 10 11 12 13 14

This book is also available on the World Wide Web as an eBook.
Visit www.abc-clio.com for details.

Libraries Unlimited
An Imprint of ABC-CLIO, LLC

ABC-CLIO, LLC
130 Cremona Drive, P.O. Box 1911
Santa Barbara, California 93116-1911

This book is printed on acid-free paper ∞
Manufactured in the United States of America

Contents

List of Illustrations

Acknowledgments

The reason the Guided Inquiry Design Framework has an authentic voice is that many people working in schools influenced and informed our thinking. All of the examples in the book are drawn from actual school situations. The seeds of this book have been sown over many years and in our many different experiences and environments. We have been fortunate to benefit from the wisdom, knowledge, and insight of many people, far too many to acknowledge in this short introduction. People from the library world, the teaching world, and the outside world helped us.

We particularly thank Carol's students who, over the years, have created innovative school library programs based on the ISP that provided extraordinary insight into Guided Inquiry. School librarians throughout the country who have been inspired by the ISP to change their approach to learning, in turn, expanded our vision to national issues of school renewal. School librarians around the world who have taken up the ISP extended our view across international cultural boundaries. The Dewitt Wallace Library Power study (University of Wisconsin, Madison), which confirmed the importance of collaborative, integrated learning in school libraries, provided impetus for pushing us forward to develop Guided Inquiry. We are indebted to the Rutgers University Center for International Scholarship in School Libraries research team, management team, advisory board, and friends whose dedication and support continues innovative research and development on the impact of school libraries on inquiry learning.

We thank Leslie's various collaborative partners who have pushed our thinking, extended our ideas, and informed the design work represented in the following pages. The following districts and schools have been on the innovative edge of Guided Inquiry, working to implement the approach with the support of Leslie's facilitation, coaching, and leadership in professional development on inquiry. At the forefront of this work has been the Department of Educational Technology and the Department of Library Services in the Denver Public Schools (DPS), as well as many teacher leaders and school librarians of DPS; Newport News Public Schools in Virginia in their inquiry academy; Farmville Elementary International Baccalaureate School in the Los Angeles Public Schools; and Teaching with Primary Sources, Colorado, at Metropolitan State College of Denver, and their excellent inquiry-driven conferences and workshops along with the Council on 21st Century Learning. We also pay tribute to the support from Leslie's international Professional Learning Network on Twitter.

Last, we thank Ann's colleagues and partners who have helped us to think outside the school. Teachers and administrators from the District of Columbia Public Schools (DCPS) inspired many of the creative examples of inquiry and use of rich resources in the school and the community. We are especially grateful to the extraordinary educators at Oyster-Adams Bilingual School and to all the educators who took part in the Smithsonian National Air and Space Museum's Science in Pre-K program and shared their struggles and triumphs as they implemented inquiry in their DCPS preschool classes. We also thank the museum educators at the National Building Museum, those at the National Air and Space Museum, and those around the Smithsonian Institution whose excellent work is highlighted in session plans and examples throughout the book.

Introduction

Guided Inquiry is a way of thinking, learning, and teaching that changes the culture of the school into a collaborative inquiry community. This book presents a framework for designing Guided Inquiry that is tailored to the needs of the students in your school. It is a fluid, flexible model that helps you guide students through the flow of discovery in the process of learning from a variety of sources of information to prepare them for successful learning and living in the information age.

Emphasis is on the Guided Inquiry process, which has eight phases: Open, Immerse, Explore, Identify, Gather, Create, Share, Evaluate. The Guided Inquiry Design Process is based in the model of thoughts, feelings, and actions in Kuhlthau's studies of the information search process (ISP) of students. Students in the ISP studies needed time to explore information and to form a focused thesis or question before collecting information to accomplish their assignments and present their findings. As they became more experienced, they explained this as "my process" and "the way I learn." The Guided Inquiry Design Process, which is based on the ISP, gives students the time and the guidance to identify their inquiry questions. Students are guided through ways to immerse in order to gain background knowledge and to explore interesting ideas in preparation for identifying a well-formed question or topic for inquiry that directs their gathering, creating, and sharing for deep meaningful learning.

This book provides a way to rethink learning and transform schools to focus on inquiry learning so that all children become prepared for life and work in the information environment. Guided Inquiry develops academic competency, career readiness, and life skills. Students use museum resources on the web and in their community to engage in the real, interesting problems and questions that scientists, historians, and researchers are grappling with to understand our world. All students can have access to this kind of learning through the design framework presented in this book. This needn't be a rare experience for a chosen few; it can be the way schools operate and the way students learn on a regular basis.

Guided Inquiry Design: A Framework for Inquiry in Your School is the third book in the Guided Inquiry series. The first book, *Seeking Meaning: A Process Approach to Library and Information Services* (2004), provides a complete description and explanation of Kuhlthau's research on the Information Search Process that forms the basis of Guided Inquiry. The second in the series, *Guided Inquiry: Learning in the 21st Century* (2007), is the foundation of Guided Inquiry and describes what it is and why it is essential for schools in the information environment of the 21st century. This third book in the series describes how to design and implement Guided Inquiry in schools.

Guided Inquiry Design: A Framework for Inquiry in Your School is authored by a team that crosses educational specializations. This team is a model of the learning team recommended in the book. Carol Kuhlthau conducted research in schools and libraries over several decades and is an expert in school libraries. Leslie Maniotes is the master teacher and curriculum specialist on the team who also contributed her research in the importance of third space in literacy learning. Ann Caspari is the outside expert who brought her knowledge of informal learning environments, museums, and community resources to broaden and extend learning outside the walls of the classroom, the library, and the school.

The three of us, from our varying perspectives on education, recognize that findings from ISP research are not being broadly implemented in schools in ways that give students power and knowledge for success in the complex information environment. We recognize that without this knowledge, students can spin within their frustrations and sabotage their own creative projects. We also see that too often the "so what?" is missing from school learning. Although projects may be well intended, the learning is more meaningful and relevant when teachers work together, have knowledge of inquiry learning, consider how the learning can be transferred to real life, and guide their students into making those kinds of connections. Students in Guided Inquiry learn to use their community resources and take advantage of informal learning opportunities that museum objects and exhibitions offer, just as they will continue to do after graduation.

This book is arranged and organized to be a practical tool to use for implementing Guided Inquiry in schools. *Guided Inquiry: Learning in 21st Century* is the companion text to this book. The two books are to be read and used together. The foundation and rationale for Guided Inquiry is laid out in that book. This book follows as how to design and implement Guided Inquiry in your school.

The first three chapters provide an overview of the design framework for the Guided Inquiry Design Process. The first chapter describes the eight phases of the Guided Inquiry process. The chapter explains how literacy, content, and social learning are interwoven into the process and it describes the learning team for guiding the inquiry.

The second chapter is a summary of the research that grounds Guided Inquiry. First, is the ISP that describes students' process of learning from a variety of sources of information in school research projects. For a full description of this research, read the first book in the Guided Inquiry series, *Seeking Meaning: A Process Approach to Library and Information Services.* Second, is the study of third space that reveals the impact of drawing students' real-world experience outside of school into their inside school curricular learning.

The third chapter introduces the five tools of inquiry that are essential to implementation. These tools are gradually introduced to students and used throughout the Guided Inquiry Design Process.

The following eight chapters, which make up the bulk of the text, are examples and explanations of the Guided Inquiry Design Process. Each chapter details one of the eight phases of the Design Process from Open to Evaluate and explains when to introduce the tools of inquiry and what teachers and students are doing during that phase. It also provides examples of inquiry at all levels from pre-K through 12th grade. Embedded in each chapter is a sample session plan for that phase that is meant as a springboard for your creative ideas.

We conclude the book with Building Guided Inquiry in Your School. It is our greatest hope that the pockets of Guided Inquiry collaborations that are currently happening between school librarians and teachers with support of administrators throughout the country will grow into a network of Inquiry Schools. With the advent of the Common Core State Standards and American Association of School Librarians 2007 Standards, educators have a clear direction toward integrated learning and movement to teach all students to be independent learners who understand their own strengths and weaknesses and can work both individually and collaboratively to contribute to a democratic society and the global information economy. It seems this blossoming network and development of an inquiry approach is timely and of the essence for students in schools today.

Guided Inquiry Design: The Process, the Learning, and the Team

Guided Inquiry Process

All children need schools that inspire, motivate, and prepare them for successful living in today's challenging information environment. The Guided Inquiry process, grounded in research on learning, provides educators with a framework for designing pre-K to 12th grade inquiry that prepares students for the workplace, citizenship, and daily living. When schools use this framework, students gain deep understanding of curriculum content and also internalize an inquiry process that they can use in academic settings, the work world, and everyday life as they apply the same inquiry strategies in the complex information environment.

We need to rethink 21st century schools so that they become more efficient and effective in the information age. Learning content in isolation is an inefficient, outdated practice. Some teachers continue to work in the isolated silos of the 20th century. Because students cannot possibly learn all of the content that is known, learning how to learn and understanding one's own learning process are more important than ever before. Learning through inquiry is relevant and authentic because it is integrated just like the real world outside of school. The Guided Inquiry design framework offers a way of teaching many things at the same time within a meaningful and integrated context. Five distinct kinds of learning, which are explained in this chapter, are intentionally interwoven throughout the inquiry process so that students gradually develop a familiarity and fluency in their own learning process.

To do this, schools need to be transformed into a collaborative culture around learning. Excellent schools of the 21st century are inquiry communities where all members are learners and the focus is on learning. The Guided Inquiry process is built around a team approach within a collaborative culture. A collaborative culture occurs when the schedule is configured around learning, specializations of personnel are considered assets to the community of learners, and priorities are placed on building intellectual and social capacities. We are expanding the idea of the core learning team from *Guided Inquiry: Learning in the 21st Century* to include an extended team of experts from inside and outside the school.

Phases of the Guided Inquiry Process

The Guided Inquiry process (Figure 1.1) begins with Open the inquiry to catch students' attention, get them thinking, and help them make connections with the world outside of school.

1

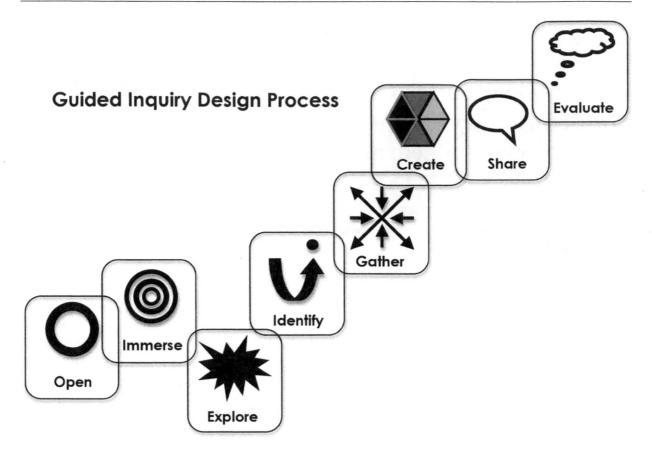

Figure 1.1 Guided Inquiry Design Process

Next is Immerse, which is designed to build enough background knowledge to generate some interesting ideas to investigate. Then Explore those ideas for an important, authentic engaging inquiry question. Next, pause to Identify and clearly articulate the inquiry question before moving on to Gather information. After gathering, Create and Share what students have learned and then Evaluate to reflect on content and process and evaluate achievement of learning. The process is not a linear one: inquiry is a "messy" process. Guided Inquiry is designed to encourage collaborative construction of knowledge with reflection and assessment of learning occurring throughout the process.

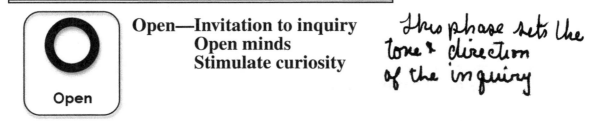

Open—Invitation to inquiry
Open minds
Stimulate curiosity

This phase sets the tone & direction of the inquiry

Open is the invitation to inquiry, the beginning of the inquiry process. Open is a distinct and important phase of the process that sets the tone and direction of the inquiry. Once the learning

[handwritten: examples of an opener?!]

team has decided on the learning goals, they need to create a powerful opener that invites the *[handwritten: ?]* learners in, establishes an inquiry stance, and introduces the general topic to engage the inquiry community.

The main goal is to open students' minds and stimulate their curiosity. The Open session inspires students to want to pursue the inquiry. The opener is designed to spark conversations about ideas and themes, pose questions and problems, and highlight concepts related to the subject. These conversations stimulate students to think about the overall content of the inquiry and to connect with what they already know from their experience and personal knowledge.

**Immerse—Build background knowledge
Connect to content
Discover interesting ideas**

[handwritten: → essential for student understanding]

In the Immerse phase, the inquiry community builds background knowledge together through an immersion experience. The learning team designs engaging ways for students to immerse in the overall ideas of the content area under study, for example, reading a book, story, or article together; viewing a video; or visiting a museum.

The main task of Immerse is to guide students to connect with the content and to discover interesting ideas to explore further. Learners are guided to think about what they already know and what seems particularly interesting, curious, surprising, or troubling. As they build background knowledge, students reflect on ideas that matter to them and are worth further investigation.

[handwritten: what is the difference? how is this done?]

**Explore—Explore interesting ideas
Look around
Dip in**

In the Explore phase of Guided Inquiry, students browse through various sources of information to explore interesting ideas and prepare to develop their inquiry questions. In this critical early phase of constructing new learning, students need to <u>explore ideas rather than accumulate facts</u>. The learning team guides students to browse and scan a variety of sources. Students dip into a few sources to make sense of the information they find and raise lots of new questions.

In the Explore phase students survey a wide range of sources, read when they find something interesting, and reflect on questions that begin to shape their inquiry. Students often become overwhelmed by all the information and confused by the ideas that don't fit together. The learning team guides students to keep an open mind as they explore and reflect on new information. Guiding students through the Explore phase leads them to form a meaningful inquiry question.

Identify—Pause and ponder
Identify inquiry question
Decide direction

have to have back ground knowledge prior to asking ?'s

In Identify learners pause in the inquiry process to ask a meaningful inquiry question and form a focus. In Guided Inquiry they have had lots of preparation for this phase. Students are ready to identify an important question for their inquiry because of the time they have spent immersing and exploring to build enough background knowledge to ask many meaningful questions.

The main task of the Identify phase is for students to construct an inquiry question from the interesting ideas, pressing problems, and emerging themes they have explored in various sources of information. The team introduces strategies that enable each student to sort through information and ideas to clearly articulate a meaningful inquiry question that will frame the rest of the inquiry.

Gather—Gather important information
Go broad
Go deep

A clearly articulated question gives direction for the Gather phase. Gather sessions are designed to help students collect detailed information from a variety of sources. This information engages them in learning about their inquiry question. The learning team guides students in locating, evaluating, and using information that leads to deep learning.

The main task of the Gather phase is to guide learners to choose what is personally meaningful and compelling about their inquiry question in the information sources they find. The learning team guides students in a structured approach for managing their search. Students "go broad" to find a range of sources that are useful for understanding their inquiry question. Students also "go deep" and choose a core of the most useful sources to read closely as they find connections and gain personal understanding.

Create—Reflect on learning
Go beyond facts to make meaning
Create to communicate

After students have gathered enough information to construct their own understandings, they are ready to organize their learning into a creative presentation during the Create phase.

Creating a way to communicate what they have learned about their inquiry helps students to articulate what is important about the subject and requires them to integrate the ideas more firmly into a deep understanding. The learning team guides students to go beyond simple fact finding and reporting and to summarize, interpret, and extend the meaning of what they have learned and create a way to share what they have learned.

Create sessions are designed to guide students to reflect on all they have learned about their inquiry question, construct their own understanding, and decide what type of presentation will best represent their engaging ideas, controversies, and theories generated through the inquiry for a particular audience. The learning team guides students in creating a meaningful, interesting, clearly articulated, well-documented presentation that tells the story of what they have learned in the inquiry process.

Share—Learn from each other
Share learning
Tell your story

Share is the culminating phase in the inquiry process when students share the product they have created to show what they have learned with the other students in their inquiry community. Students have become experts on the question for their inquiry community. They now have the opportunity and responsibility to share their insights with other students and contribute their learning to others. Their inquiry products also may be shared with a wider audience, and what they have learned may result in taking an action.

Share is designed so that students share the products they have developed during Create to communicate what they have learned about their inquiry question in an interesting, informative way. An important component of Guided Inquiry is the collaborative learning that takes place when students share what they have learned in the inquiry process. The learning team organizes Share sessions to provide the best conditions for students to learn substantial content from each other.

Evaluate—Evaluate achievement of learning goals
Reflect on content
Reflect on process

The Evaluate phase, which occurs at the close of the inquiry process, is an essential component in Guided Inquiry. Although Guided Inquiry incorporates assessment for determining student progress throughout all of the phases of the inquiry process, evaluation also occurs at the end when the learning team evaluates students' achievement of the learning goals.

The learning team guides students in reflection for self-assessment of their content learning and their progress through the inquiry process. Students' self-reflection takes place while the entire process is fresh in their minds and reinforces content learning and establishes good habits for learning how to learn through the inquiry process.

Guided Inquiry Sessions

Within the larger framework of the inquiry process lies the smaller framework of inquiry sessions. Because time with students is constrained by the structure of the school day, the integrated process is divided into meaningful sessions. Guided Inquiry is conducted through inquiry sessions rather than lessons. Lessons imply teacher-directed learning where the teacher has all the answers. Sessions, in contrast, are learning centered and the team facilitates learning in an environment designed to enter the third space where the student and the curriculum meet. Sessions are designed to get students started in an engaging worktime followed by a reflection and consideration for some next steps to be taken.

Within the entire process, each phase includes multiple sessions. Throughout the book there are many models and examples of inquiry sessions. Each inquiry session consists of a starter, a worktime, and a reflection. For each phase of the Guided Inquiry process we have included at least one full session plan specifically designed for that phase in the inquiry process. There are two kinds of session plans in this book, models and examples. Model session plans are more general and exclude specific content. The example session plans are more specific to a particular unit of study. All of the session plans in this book are templates to help you create your own session plans designed for each phase of the process. Each session plan in the book features learning goals for inquiry or learning how to learn. With more experience at planning for inquiry, you will incorporate multiple and overlapping goals from the five kinds of learning in each session. To get you started, we focused here on the goals for inquiry at each phase. All of these ideas are meant for you to borrow, rework, and use. They are meant as a type of starter for you to think about all the nuances of each phase as you begin to design inquiry in your school, starting with growing students understanding of their engagement in the inquiry process.

Guided Inquiry sessions include (Figure 1.2):

- Starter
- Worktime
- Reflection

Starter: The starter gets students thinking about what they will work on during that session. Starters may be an instructional mini-lesson to teach some skill that is needed in the worktime. It may include raising questions to pursue or a problem to solve. The starter will usually be short, attention getting, and informative. As in all designed inquiry learning, the teacher carefully balances his or her talk with that of the community, being sure to always engage the learners with purpose. The starter should not have too much teacher talk but just enough to set the work of the session.

For the starter, the learning team plans together to present an opening that will engage the learners. The starter provides enough time for students to be able to converse in the whole group

SESSION PLAN

OPEN - IMMERSE - EXPLORE - IDENTIFY - GATHER - CREATE - SHARE - EVALUATE

Learning Goals:
Location:
Team:
Inquiry Unit:

Starter Time:	
Worktime Time:	
Reflection Time:	
Notes:	

Figure 1.2 Session Plan Template

From *Guided Inquiry Design: A Framework for Inquiry in Your School* by Carol C. Kuhlthau, Leslie K. Maniotes, and Ann K. Caspari. Santa Barbara, CA: Libraries Unlimited. Copyright © 2012.

and begin to become engaged with the ideas. The starter can take many forms and does not have to be limited to one type of media but should be short and engaging.

Worktime: The worktime consists of the largest chunk of time in the session. There should be ample time for students to engage the ideas and each other. Here the students may work individually, pair to share ideas, or converse in small groups to develop some of the ideas that surface. They use one of their inquiry tools to help them work out and capture their ideas. The worktime will vary with the type of activity. Students may be looking for specific information in a database. They may be working in their inquiry circle to formulate questions. A worktime may be individual study, a small group inquiry circle, or whole group sharing. The starter may take only a few minutes or it may take as much as half the session, but the starter is always followed by a worktime and a reflection. No matter how long the starter and worktime take, the session must be concluded in time to close with reflection. Keeping to this inquiry session framework is important for the success of Guided Inquiry. For example, when using an expert, a starter may be an introduction to the expert, the worktime, is the expert's story and the reflection is a discussion of what was important and new.

Reflection: The reflection may bring the whole community back together or it may occur within the inquiry circle to find the threads and commonalities in the group. The students also take time to reflect individually to carry the opening into the next session. Some prompts for reflection are: What do you wonder? What surprised you here? What did this make you think of? What did this remind you of? What's next? Reflection is essential for learning to take place. Every session closes with reflection on what was learned, what was clear, what was confusing, and where to go from here. In constructivist learning, students are introduced to a concept or problem and then have opportunities to interact with the ideas, to mess about, and to invent. Equally important to these components is a reflection on the learning that concentrates on what was learned and keeps the momentum of inquiry going by generating new thoughts for moving forward.

Five Kinds of Learning

An important advantage of Guided Inquiry is the variety of different competencies and knowledge that students develop while engaged in the inquiry process. When inquiry is guided in this way, students accomplish five interwoven, integrated kinds of learning (Figure 1.3). These are:

- Curriculum content
- Information literacy
- Learning how to learn
- Literacy competency
- Social skills

Curriculum content incorporates fact finding with interpreting and synthesizing in discipline-specific areas. Information literacy involves understanding underlying concepts for locating, evaluating, and using information. Learning how to learn develops a personal sense of the learning process. Literacy competency is the ability to apply reading, writing, speaking,

Five Kinds of Learning through Guided Inquiry	
Information Literacy	Concepts for locating, evaluating, and using information
Learning How to Learn	Self-directed learning and personal interaction within the inquiry process
Curriculum Content	Constructing new knowledge, interpreting, synthesizing, and applying facts and ideas
Literacy Competence	Reading, writing, speaking, listening, viewing, and presenting
Social Skills	Interacting, cooperating, collaborating, habits of mind, dispositions in action

Figure 1.3 Five Kinds of Learning through Guided Inquiry

listening, viewing, and presenting for learning in a variety of different formats. Social skills involve the ability to interact, cooperate, and collaborate in successful sustained group work and within a wide variety of contexts. These five kinds of learning are essential for developing academic competency, career readiness, and life skills.

Curriculum Content

All inquiry has subject content: something for students to think about, something interesting and worthwhile to investigate, something new to learn. Guided Inquiry is bound to subject area curriculum such as defined by the Common Core Standards. Student interest and engagement are critical components, but the curriculum is the starting point for defining the subject of inquiry. Inquiry broadens and deepens student understanding of a subject by going beyond fact finding into synthesizing and interpreting information, facts, and ideas. Certain subject content is better learned through inquiry than by any other method. Those areas that require open-ended questions, different perspectives and points of view, and emerging ideas and concepts are the best candidates for inquiry learning. A limited number of curriculum goals require rote memorization, but even those may be expanded and deepened by being combined with inquiry. Curriculum goals that require surveying a wide range of factual material, such as study of a period of history, are greatly enhanced when combined with inquiry that takes students deeper into a particular aspect or concept. Longitudinal studies found that the insights gained through inquiry were what students remembered long after the course of study was completed (Kuhlthau 2004). As a result of Guided Inquiry, students transfer their understanding into new contexts as they create and share learning with others.

Information Literacy

The American Association of School Librarians' *Standards for the 21st Century Learner* (2007) builds information literacy around inquiry learning. Guided Inquiry applies a concepts approach to information literacy rather than a skills approach (Kuhlthau, Maniotes, and Caspari 2007). This means that students learn the underlying concepts of locating, evaluating, and using information that are transferable to a wide range of situations. Information literacy is integrated into each stage of the inquiry process and emphasized in the Explore and Gather phases. Locating information is easier with the new understanding of each new technological development and search tool. But evaluation is more important than ever because the Internet has become a general source of information. Information literacy is the ability to make wise judgments about information. By daily practice in investigating, comparing, reflecting, and discussing, students develop habits of mind and ways of thinking critically about information. Information literacy is a way of thinking rather than a set of skills. The concepts of information literacy are practical and usable even as technology changes. The fundamental concept of using information is to go beyond fact finding to seek meaning for accomplishing a goal. Guided Inquiry enables students to ask meaningful questions, locate and evaluate quality information, manage inquiry, interpret facts, and organize ideas for creating and sharing their learning with others.

Learning How to Learn

Guided Inquiry is based in the process of learning how to learn from a variety of sources of information and is fundamental for success in the 21st century. Students develop a sense of their own learning by working through the phases of the inquiry process. Students gain an understanding that emotions and affect play a key role in learning and understanding and ideas do not come together easily on their own. They learn strategies and structures for managing inquiry through guidance provided at critical intervention points. During Explore students are guided to browse and dip in, mull and explore more widely as a strategy to ease their uncertainty. They learn that it is natural and normal not to know everything at this point and that they need to tolerate feelings of confusion without frustration. Students develop the independent learning abilities that are required for academic competency and college readiness that, unfortunately, many students are lacking today. This learning translates into life. Guided Inquiry is a fundamental way of learning in the information environment of the world outside the school where everyday tasks require learning from a variety of sources of information for decision-making, problem solving, and critical thinking. Learning how to learn also prepares students for creating and innovating in a complex changing workplace.

Literacy Competency

High levels of literacy are required of the 21st century learner. Guided Inquiry puts literacy into action. Students actively read, view, write, listen, speak, and present throughout the inquiry process. Competency builds in each area with intensive application and use. Students go beyond learning to read, to reading to learn. Guided Inquiry supports the comprehension of informational texts as well as fiction. Determining importance in a variety of informational texts (images, objects, videos, multimedia formats, web pages, and a variety of other written sources) is an essential skill in the information environment in which students live and learn. Every aspect of literacy, reading, writing, speaking, listening, viewing, and presenting, is developed throughout the inquiry process. The best way to become proficient in each of the literacy competencies is to practice, practice, practice. Students' literacy competence builds in Guided Inquiry through sustained, challenging, comprehensive application in an engaging inquiry community.

Social Skills

Guided Inquiry is organized around a community of learners that is referred to as an inquiry community. Social interaction among students is an essential component of the construction of understanding and learning through the inquiry process. Individual student learning takes place in an interactive group environment in both large and small groups. Social skills develop interactive collaboration throughout the stages of the inquiry process. Students need to know what is expected of them and to value the interaction as an important way of learning. Success depends on a considerable degree of cooperation, including building structures that support mutual respect for each other's ideas. All learning happens in a social context and Guided Inquiry employs the social contexts to enhance and enrich the learning. The learning team guides students to develop mutually agreed upon standards of behavior for the inquiry community. These clearly articulated standards form the normal way of conducting and proceeding as they build social skills for interacting, cooperating, and collaborating in productive work groups. Schools are unique communities where students have opportunities to experience extensive face-to-face interaction that is often lacking in today's technologically saturated environment. Schools that provide healthy inquiry communities where interaction is dynamic and challenging gradually build a broad range of vital social skills.

Organizing the Guided Inquiry Learning Team

A flexible team approach is a central component of the Guided Inquiry design. Guided Inquiry occurs in schools that have a collaborative culture. Three-member core learning teams are recommended to plan and supervise the inquiry, with an extended team of other experts invited to join in when needed. The main purpose of teaming is to take full advantage of the expertise in the school and community. Flexible teams of teachers and school librarians with varied expertise are formed and adapted according to the curriculum requirements of a particular unit of study and the needs of a specific group of students. The learning team is reconstituted with each inquiry unit, and adjustments are made according to the changes in curriculum and students needs. Guided Inquiry learning teams are flexible and organized around the students' specific learning goals and needs.

The Core Learning Team

Organizing around a three-member core team brings a synergy of ideas and specialized expertise for developing inquiry learning and for guiding the inquiry process. Although two-member learning teams made up of a teacher and a school librarian are common and can be effective, three-member teams are highly recommended wherever possible and practical.

The advantage of a three-member team is an increase in the ability to teach the five kinds of learning as well as integrate ideas across different curriculum content areas. Although knowledge and understanding cut across subject areas and the great challenges of our time require integration of all kinds of thinking and learning, teaching often stays in the convenient silos of discipline and expertise. Each core team member brings a particular area of specialization and expertise in one of the five kinds of learning. The school librarian is an expert in information literacy and also the resource specialist on the team. The school librarian's expertise in teaching students to locate, evaluate, and use a variety of sources for learning is integrated into each phase of the inquiry process. The teacher, an elementary classroom teacher or a subject area teacher in middle and secondary school, works as the curriculum content expert. The teacher as the content expert and school librarian as the expert on information literacy, resources, and technology are essential members of the core team.

The third core team member may add value to the curriculum content and integration of ideas across content areas. In this case, the third member might be a teacher with specialization in the arts or an affiliated subject area. The third core team member may have specialized teaching expertise in one of the other kinds of learning. A literacy specialist may join the team to help students improve their reading and writing. An English as a Second Language (ESL) teacher may join to meet the language needs of a specific group of students. A social worker, school counselor, or guidance expert may be asked to join the team to focus on social skills if the project and group require extra intervention. In addition, all team members bring expertise in developing students' social skills and their understanding of learning how to learn.

Three-member core teams provide the additional professional guidance and ongoing support for students that Guided Inquiry requires. However, more is not necessarily better on the learning team. Larger teams tend to be cumbersome with too much going on and they are not as effective for guiding student learning. Too many subject areas with diverse objectives may merely clutter and confuse the inquiry, actually obstructing rather than enhancing learning (Kuhlthau 2004, p. 155). It is important to find the right balance of achievable goals and integrated content and processes for effective learning to take place. Teams working together provide the additional guidance and support needed to teach and assess the five kinds of learning throughout the inquiry process to a specific group of students with particular goals for learning. There will most likely be one person who initiates the process. However, once the team is established, each member will take leadership roles in line with their expertise.

The Extended Learning Team

The core learning team provides guidance and instruction throughout the inquiry process. The extended team adds expertise when needed. It is a good idea to identify who might be invited to join the extended team early in the process in order to give these extended team members a chance to plan and become engaged in learning goals of the inquiry as well.

The core learning team considers what other expertise will enhance the inquiry and who should be invited to join the extended team to provide that expertise. Extended team members are brought in at critical points in the inquiry process to provide expertise and experience that enhance student thinking and learning. These critical points are identified throughout the book. Experts within the school may be invited to add a particular piece of instruction and content.

For example, in designing the Immerse session for exploring shadows in a preschool class, the learning team of teacher, school librarian, and science specialist found it helpful to have the specialized help of an extended team member working with the learning team to facilitate small group work. The extended team may be employed at this time to help guide each inquiry circle as needed. In this case the teacher asked the ESL teacher to come in during one of her sessions and work with a group of primarily Spanish-speaking students when they were experimenting with flashlights and shadow boxes. This meant the learning team included a teacher, a school librarian, and a science specialist with an ESL teacher joining as an extended team member. The students with language barriers who were usually very quiet were engaged with the ESL teacher to facilitate learning. The simple experiments provided an opportunity for everyone to expand vocabulary and learn new words and ideas in both languages for English Language Development (ELD).

In other examples for older students, a technology teacher may join the extended team for one or two sessions to help students edit and publish video or create presentation in a web-based sharing tool. An art teacher may join the extended team for one or two sessions to help students design products of inquiry and understand aesthetics or a particular art process, such as poster design or model making. A school counselor may be asked to contribute some sessions on effective collaboration or listening skills for an inquiry environment. A drama or music teacher may present an immersion experience and help students explore how ideas can be expressed through the arts.

The result of this team approach is that students are supported in all aspects of learning so that they may more easily understand the interconnected nature of the learning process. Process and content are intertwined and not taught independently. For example, if an inquiry community decides to create DNA models as a product of an extensive inquiry process, they may benefit from the expertise of an art teacher and a technology expert, as well as the science teacher and school librarian. Students will need to learn how to make models from different materials, why scientists use models to understand complex objects, and how to find examples of models that have been designed to explore DNA, as well as the components of DNA and how they work together. This kind of deep and complex learning is better done by a collaborative learning team than one or two teachers alone.

The Extended Team from the Community

Targeting a specific, related aspect of a resource at the outset helps in the planning phase to get dates on the calendar and make needed contacts as the inquiry progresses. The extended team also may incorporate community members to generate authentic experiences. Experts outside of the school may be invited to share their personal experience related to the inquiry area of study.

Experts from outside the school can enhance the inquiry learning at different points in the process. Immersion experiences are enhanced by authentic experiences that can often be provided within the community such as a visit to a museum or field site or a visit from someone with a personal story. Experts as extended team members from the community, such as a museum educator, field guide, or expert speaker such as an architect or journalist, enhance the inquiry unit. Public librarians are a welcome help during the Gather phase of the inquiry process. When you think of community experts as members of the extended team you are more likely to give them the background they need to tailor their contribution to your students and the specifics of their inquiry. Experts are more interesting and effective when they have time to prepare, are aware of the scope of the inquiry, and can address the students' specific goals.

The extended team may incorporate personnel from cultural or civic organizations such as libraries, museums, zoos, historical sites, and nature parks. These community resources offer a wealth of information, and the staff can provide both subject matter expertise and expertise in methodology used to examine objects in the collection. These might be primary or secondary sources, ephemera, historic photos, or teaching collections of real objects or authentic reproductions. Each resource has specific strategies that can be used to uncover the unique information they possess.

Too often we isolate ourselves in school and do not use the local resources around us to improve the school experience. Guided Inquiry and the inclusion of the extended team expand learning into these local resources. A museum field trip that doesn't lead to an inquiry is a missed opportunity for learning. Although most schools are not systematically tied to museums or other local programs, teachers and school librarians are increasingly taking advantage of the rich resources and lessons created by museums and other community educational institutions. Often lessons are available that are tied to standards and can fit right into what is being taught. These types of lessons take an inquiry stance or approach. Unfortunately, these types of experiences often stand alone and are not integrated into inquiry learning. When used as an immersion experience that leads to the next step of integrating the learning into the student's personal understanding, these experiences are tools for inquiry. It is the task of the learning team to connect to the extended team and make connections that will broaden the scope of learning.

Resources for Guided Inquiry

Guided Inquiry requires a wide range of interesting, challenging print and electronic resources for learning, as well as a rich environment of objects, experts, and experiences. Drawing community resources into the school is an important component of Guided Inquiry. Engaging experiences make inquiry meaningful, interesting, and relevant. School learning often seems removed from the world outside the walls of the school. The community is filled with resources that are ready to be tapped to enhance learning. Museums, historical sites, natural habitats, personal collections, expert stories, and talent can capture the students' imagination and inspire them to want to know more. The above section also describes how Guided Inquiry thoughtfully integrates these resources through the inquiry process at phases when they are most meaningful for students.

The Internet opens up a wealth of valuable resources for inquiry learning. However, the Internet is a massive mix of information, much of which is irrelevant, misleading, inappropriate, and overwhelming for school learning. School librarians are transforming school libraries into digital libraries to provide the specific resources that are essential for inquiry learning. The school digital library incorporates digitized materials, including museum collections, archives, and selected web sites, databases, and e-books with books and audio and video materials, as well as contacts with people who have relevant expertise and first-hand experience. All resources are directly related to the curriculum and tailored to students' developmental capacity and learning needs.

An essential role of the school librarian on the learning team is as the resource specialist who opens access to a variety of quality resources to support student learning in the phases of the inquiry process. In the past, school librarians served as resource providers, collecting and organizing materials to enhance the curriculum that was housed in the school library. Today school librarians serve as resource specialists, enabling access to a wide range of resources both inside and outside of the school for learning in all areas of the curriculum. The school librarian has expertise in designing and guiding learning from a variety of sources of information and for scaffolding these resources through the inquiry process. As resource specialists, school librarians have expertise in social networking technology, such as wikis, blogs, and other tools for collaborating and communicating in the inquiry process.

School Librarians in Information Age Learning

The evolution of the role of school libraries follows the evolution of changes in education in the information age. School librarians are vital agents who create schools that enable students to learn through vast resources and multiple communication channels in a complex information environment. They have the specialized training and expertise in teaching students how to locate, evaluate, and use information. They have broad knowledge of the extensive resources in the library, on the Internet, and in the community. They have the expertise to provide a digital library to supplement in-school resources specifically tailored to the inquiry unit. They have flexible collaboration and managerial skills to transform the school into an inquiry community. They coordinate the inquiry projects, arrange for the extended team, and, as one principal aptly put it, "keep things going." As team collaborator, the school librarian draws people in and keeps things on track.

What's Next? The Research

A unique characteristic of Guided Inquiry among educational approaches is that it is grounded in sound research. It is a truly research-based program and design. The research came first out of a problem from the practical setting in schools. The design grew out of the application of returning the research back to the practical setting. In the next chapter, Guided Inquiry's research basis is clearly described and explained. Guided Inquiry uniquely crosses educational fields by using the research that Carol Kuhlthau conducted in the field of library studies and information science, as well as Leslie Maniotes's research in the importance of third space in literacy learning. Ann Caspari lends her expertise in the use of informal learning environments, museums, and community resources to broaden and extend learning outside the walls of the classroom and school.

The Research Behind the Design

The Guided Inquiry Design Framework is grounded in the findings of two major areas of research on learning. First, is the Information Search Process (ISP) that describes students' process of learning from a variety of information sources in school research projects. Second is the study of third space that reveals the impact of drawing students' real-world experience outside of school into their inside-school curricular learning. The first section of this chapter explains how the Guided Inquiry design framework was built around the model of the ISP, which describes students' experience in six stages of information seeking and learning. The second section describes how third space, which is where the students' world and the curriculum meet, is the "watermark" of Guided Inquiry underlying each phase in the inquiry process.

Inside the Inquiry Process: What the Information Search Process Tells Us About Guiding and Intervening

The ISP was discovered and developed over several decades of research on students' process of learning from a variety of information sources (Kuhlthau 1985, 2004). These studies from the students' perspective investigated their thoughts, actions, and feelings while they were involved in extensive research projects. When were they having difficulty? Why were they having difficulty? When were they experiencing success? Why did they experience success? Were there times when they needed help? What kind of help would be useful?

Students progressed through the following six identifiable stages, which are named for the main task to be accomplished in each stage, plus a seventh stage of assessment:

□ *These studies from the students' perspective investigated their thoughts, actions, and feelings while they were involved in extensive research projects.*

17

- **Initiation:** initiating a research project
- **Selection:** selecting a topic
- **Exploration:** exploring for focus
- **Formulation:** formulating a focus
- **Collection:** collecting information on focus
- **Presentation:** preparing to present
- **Assessment:** assessing the process

(Kuhlthau 1985, p. 25)

□ An important finding in these studies is that thoughts were charged with emotions that influenced the actions students took. Feelings were important and indicated when students were having difficulty and when they were doing well on their own.

Students were studied in each stage of the research process to investigate their feelings (affective), thoughts (cognitive), and actions (physical). An important finding in these studies is that thoughts were charged with emotions that influenced the actions students took. Feelings were important and indicated when students were having difficulty and when they were doing well on their own. Students often expected to be able to simply collect information and complete the task. This simple view of the research process set up stumbling blocks, especially in the Exploration and Formulation stages. When their expectations did not match what they were experiencing, students became confused, anxious, and frustrated. Students in these studies commonly experienced a dip in confidence and an increase in uncertainty when least expected, that is, during the Exploration stage. Kuhlthau's model of the ISP describes students' interconnected thoughts, feelings, and actions in a series of six stages and shows a turning point in the Formulation stage (Kuhlthau 2004; Figure 2.1).

□ The model of the ISP was confirmed and expanded in successive studies, which revealed it to be a common experience of not only students but people in the workplace and other areas of life in which extensive information seeking and learning was involved.

The model of the ISP was confirmed and expanded in successive studies, which revealed it to be a common experience of not only students but people in the workplace and other areas of life in which extensive information seeking and learning was involved (Kuhlthau 2004). Recent studies of inquiry learning conducted at the Center for International Scholarship in School Libraries at Rutgers University (Todd, Kuhlthau, and Heinstrom 2005; Todd, Gordon, and Lu 2010) found that the model of the ISP continues to apply in technological information environments. The ISP provides an insider's view of the inquiry process that gives a clear sense of when to intervene and what guidance is most helpful. It also shows what can go wrong without informed intervention.

Over the years this research has changed the way many librarians and teachers help students with research assignments. It has opened a pathway to know what students are experiencing when they are constructing new understandings and learning from multiple sources in the dynamic information environment.

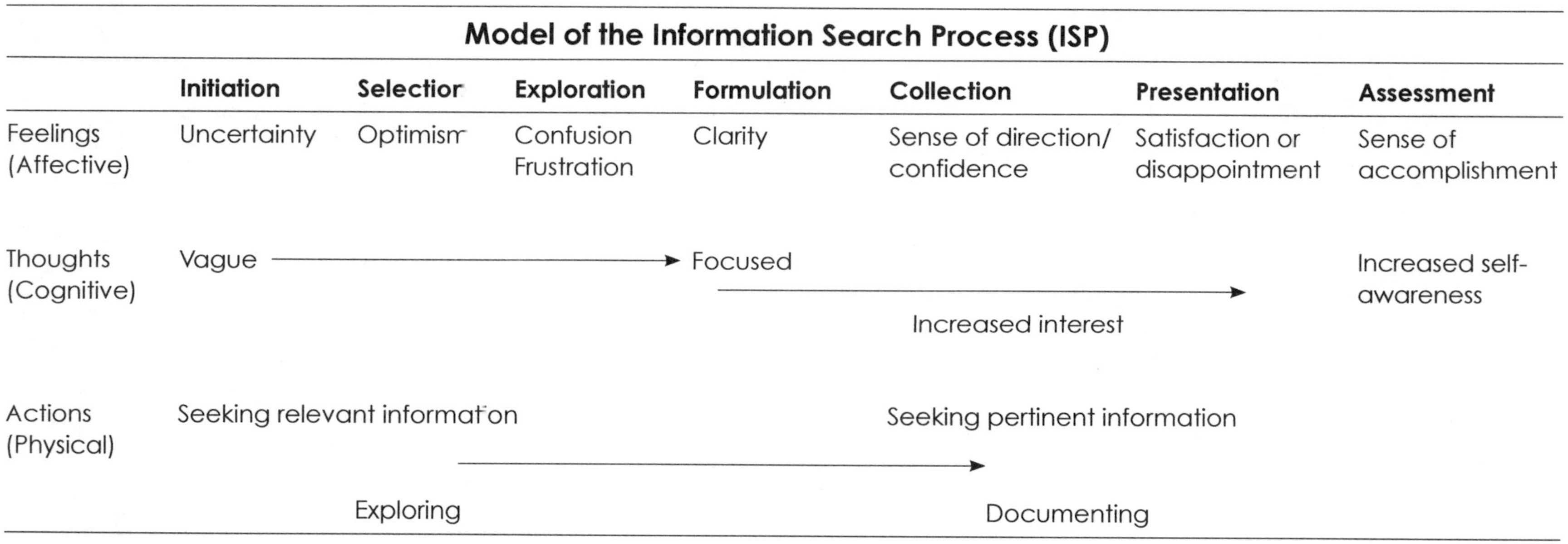

Model of the Information Search Process (ISP)

	Initiation	Selection	Exploration	Formulation	Collection	Presentation	Assessment
Feelings (Affective)	Uncertainty	Optimism	Confusion Frustration	Clarity	Sense of direction/ confidence	Satisfaction or disappointment	Sense of accomplishment
Thoughts (Cognitive)	Vague ————————————————→ Focused				————————————→ Increased interest		Increased self-awareness
Actions (Physical)	Seeking relevant information ————————————————→ Exploring				Seeking pertinent information ————————→ Documenting		

Kuhlthau (2004, p. 82)

Figure 2.1 Model of the Information Search Process

□ *Students need considerable guidance and intervention throughout the research process to construct a personal understanding. Without guidance, they tend to approach the process as a simple collecting and presenting assignment that leads to copying and pasting with little real learning.*

The ISP studies revealed that students need considerable guidance and intervention throughout the research process to construct a personal understanding. Without guidance, they tend to approach the process as a simple collecting and presenting assignment that leads to copying and pasting with little real learning. With guidance, they are able to construct new knowledge in the stages of the ISP and gain personal understanding and transferable skills.

Zone of Intervention in the Information Search Process

The research showed that each stage of the ISP called for a different type of assistance and guidance. It also became obvious that students didn't need someone hovering over them all the time. They needed help at certain times and to be on their own at other times. With this idea in mind, the concept of a zone of intervention was modeled on Vygotsky's zone of proximal development (Kuhlthau 2004). Guidance is developed around a zone of intervention when a student can do with advice and assistance what he or she cannot do alone or can do only with great difficulty. The total experience of students in each stage of the ISP informs teachers and librarians of when and how to guide students' learning through each stage of the inquiry process. The Guided Inquiry Design Framework sets up the learning environment with intervention at times when students need it and independence when they don't (Kuhlthau 2004, p. 129; Figure 2.2).

□ *Each stage of the ISP called for a different type of assistance and guidance.*

□ *The ISP was depicted on a timeline to show a process that moves in time.*

The ISP was depicted on a timeline to show a process that moves in time; like all of life's processes, there is a beginning, middle, and end. Of course, the ISP is experienced multidimensionally with thoughts, actions, and feelings that change throughout the process, also shown on the timeline. The advantage of this timeline is that it helps visualize the whole process in one summary chart.

□ *Our goal in Guided Inquiry is to make a student's vague, unformed, sometimes mistaken thinking into a clear, deep personal understanding.*

Our goal in Guided Inquiry is to make a student's vague, unformed, sometimes mistaken thinking into a clear, deep personal understanding. A good way to describe this process is in

Zone of Intervention
That area in which a student can do with advice and assistance what he or she cannot do alone or can do only with great difficulty.

Figure 2.2 Definition of the Zone of Intervention

stages or phases from the earliest unformed thoughts to the completion in deep learning. The best way to guide this process is to design targeted intervention that helps students to accomplish the tasks in each of the phases from beginning to end. Without this sustained guidance, students can flounder and go astray at any point. Guided Inquiry is designed to ensure that students have the sustained guidance they need throughout the inquiry process. Some people think of the ISP timeline as a roller coaster ride. When describing it to your students, you may find that you are waving your hand in a circular motion while moving it along in front of you. So perhaps the ISP is more like a "moving circular motion time ride with a dip in the middle." However you choose to describe the ISP, you will need to stress the evolving, holistic experience of learning in the inquiry process. Based in the ISP, the Guided Inquiry design framework is a phased approach with tasks to be accomplished in each phase that support students' feeling, thoughts, and actions in the process of learning.

☐ *Based in the ISP, the Guided Inquiry Design Framework is a phased approach with tasks to be accomplished in each phase that support students' feeling, thoughts, and actions in the process of learning.*

Stages of the Information Search Process

The next section of this chapter is a more in-depth description of the thoughts, feelings, and actions that occurred in each stage of the ISP: Initiation, Selection, Exploration, Formulation, Collection, Presentation, and Assessment. Discussion of the zone of intervention in each stage shows how the Guided Inquiry Design Framework builds on this research to provide intervention and guidance by the learning team for each phase in the inquiry process.

Initiation: Initiating a Research Assignment

In the Initiation stage of the ISP, the teacher announced a research assignment that required information from a variety of sources to be accomplished over a number of weeks. The students' task in this first stage was to think about a topic for research. Students often felt apprehensive and uncertain about what was expected of them and overwhelmed at the amount of work ahead. Talking with other classmates about requirements was a natural action to take, but some felt they should be "going it alone" and that checking with others might not be "entirely fair." Insights from the Initiation stage of the ISP are important to consider for designing the Open phase of Guided Inquiry.

☐ *Students often felt apprehensive and uncertain about what was expected of them and overwhelmed at the amount of work ahead.*

The zone of intervention indicated in the ISP for Opening Guided Inquiry is to open the conversation about the inquiry,

□ Making sure that students understand that it is not only fair to talk about their ideas and questions, it is necessary to have these conversations at this phase.

making sure that students understand that it is not only fair to talk about their ideas and questions, it is necessary to have these conversations at this phase. In this book we describe how to develop an inquiry community that forms a supportive environment for the inquiry process. Rather than simply announcing a research assignment, teachers using Guided Inquiry open with big ideas and overarching themes, perhaps through a stimulating video that opens minds and captures attention. The Open phase draws students in to think about what they already know, care about, and are curious to know more about. In Guided Inquiry, the only "going it alone" is for each student to think about what is personally important and interesting about the inquiry.

Selection: Selecting a Topic

In the Selection stage of the ISP, students selected their research topic within the subject area of the assignment. Before students selected a general topic, they were confused and somewhat anxious. After they made the choice, they often experienced a brief sense of elation, followed by apprehension at the extent of the task ahead. Feelings were quite evident in the Selection stage of the ISP. Many students wanted to select a topic quickly and dive right into collecting information and completing the research.

□ Many students wanted to select a topic quickly and dive right into collecting information and completing the research.

The Selection stage involved a zone of intervention that was not being met. Students frequently were selecting topics with little background knowledge. Although some felt relieved, even briefly elated, when they settled on a topic, they often were not prepared for the difficulties ahead. In a similar way, many inquiry approaches start by requiring students to come up with an inquiry question. A typical inquiry project begins with a brainstorming session to elicit questions from the class, then each student chooses one of the questions to investigate. Students need lots of groundwork before they can form meaningful questions that they want to pursue and are worth investigating.

□ Students need lots of groundwork before they can form meaningful questions that they want to pursue and are worth investigating.

In Guided Inquiry, identifying the inquiry question is the fourth phase in the inquiry process. Guided Inquiry is designed to develop students' ability to ask questions that are meaningful and worthy of inquiry through Immerse and Explore. The interventions and guidance in these early phases of Guided Inquiry provide the essential preparation for successful inquiry learning. In preparation for forming important questions, students build background knowledge to discover interesting ideas. Rather than rushing into asking a question, Guided Inquiry immerses students in background knowledge as an important phase in their learning process. The learning team designs engaging ways for students to immerse in the background information and big ideas of the

□ In preparation for forming important questions, students build background knowledge to discover interesting ideas.

content area under study, perhaps by a museum visit, using historical fiction, or a science experiment. This is an important area for intervention. Students benefit from immersing in the general topic that increases their background knowledge and introduces interesting ideas for further inquiry.

Exploration: Exploring for Focus

In the Exploration stage of the ISP, the students' task was to explore information on the general topic with the intent of finding a focus. As students explored information about their topics, they frequently became confused by the inconsistencies and incompatibilities of information in sources with different perspectives and differing points of view. Information didn't match their preconceived notions about their topics, and feelings of confusion and uncertainty often became frustrating. Some students wanted to drop their topics at that point. For most students this was the most difficult stage of the ISP. Students often expressed annoyance that they weren't moving along more quickly and felt they were procrastinating. When information didn't fit together or match what they expected, they had the sense that something was going wrong. They were confronted with the complicated task of working through the facts and ideas to form a focused perspective to pursue. But many thought they were merely collecting information on their topic and hurriedly copied text without giving much thought to the ideas they were encountering. The ISP studies found that a common student problem was that they skipped over the Exploration and Formulation stages and attempted to move on to the Collection stage without having formed a focus for their research.

The ISP shows Exploration is another zone of intervention when students need support, structure, and strategies for learning from different perspectives, assimilating new ideas, and forming a focus from these ideas. They also need to understand the difference between exploring for interesting ideas and collecting detailed information. Guided Inquiry is designed to build this type of support, structure, and strategy for exploring interesting ideas in preparation for identifying an important inquiry question. Without intervention, students become confused about the purpose of the Explore phase of the inquiry process and can easily become frustrated and discouraged. Guided Inquiry provides encouragement along with strategies for locating and evaluating information and guidance in reading, reflecting, and making sense of information that leads to asking fruitful inquiry questions. At the close of the Explore phase, students are ready to identify a meaningful inquiry question.

☐ *As students explored information about their topics, they frequently became confused by the inconsistencies and incompatibilities of information in sources with different perspectives and differing points of view.*

☐ *The ISP studies found that a common student problem was that they skipped over the Exploration and Formulation stages and attempted to move on to the Collection stage without having formed a focus for their research.*

☐ *Students need support, structure, and strategies for learning from different perspectives, assimilating new ideas, and forming a focus from these ideas. They also need to understand the difference between exploring for interesting ideas and collecting detailed information.*

An Important Finding: Focus Is the Turning Point

☐ *The formulation of a focus was a turning point in the research process.*

Another important finding from the ISP studies that has major implications for the Guided Inquiry Design Framework is that the formulation of a focus was a turning point in the research process. There was a distinct difference between the experience of students who formed a focus for the Collection stage and those who did not. Students who did not identify a focus in the Formulation stage and continued to collect information on the general topic had difficulty writing their research paper (Kuhlthau 2004). One student explained that she kept collecting interesting ideas but didn't ever form a focus for her topic. When she started to write her paper, she experienced a writing block. Here's how she described her difficulty in writing a paper without forming a focus in the Formulation stage:

☐ *Students who did not identify a focus in the Formulation stage and continued to collect information on the general topic had difficulty writing their research paper.*

> I had a general idea, not a specific focus, but an idea. As I was writing, I didn't know what my focus was. My teacher says she doesn't know what my focus was. I don't think I ever acquired a focus. It was an impossible paper to write. I would just sit there and say, 'I'm stuck.' There was no outline because there was nothing to complete. If I learned anything from that paper it is, you have to have a focus. You have to have something to center on. You can't just have a topic. You should have an idea when you start. I had a topic but I didn't know what I wanted to do with it. I figured that when I did my research it would focus in. But I didn't let it. I kept saying this is interesting and this is interesting and I'll just smush it all together. It didn't work out.
>
> (Kuhlthau 1994, p. 55)

☐ *There is a critical zone of intervention in the middle of the ISP that helped students to prepare for the writing process at the end.*

These studies found that there is a critical zone of intervention in the middle of the ISP that helped students to prepare for the writing process at the end. The focus they formed in the Formulation stage enabled them to develop their thoughts in the Collection stage for writing in the Presentation stage. Without a focus, they collected lots of information but hadn't thought much about how the information would fit together or what it meant.

☐ *The ISP and the writing process are very closely related. In fact, the ISP is actually preparation for the writing process. It is the way students learn from information and formulate ideas to write about.*

The ISP and the writing process are very closely related. In fact, the ISP is actually preparation for the writing process. It is the way students learn from information and formulate ideas to write about. These studies confirmed that writing blocks were thinking blocks where students hadn't formulated their thoughts sufficiently to be ready to write. The stages of ISP merge with the prewriting phase of the writing process. The student quoted above described a thinking block that resulted in a writing block.

Because she hadn't formed a focus in the Formulation stage, she continued to collect general information that wasn't centered on any particular focus. She could only report on the disparate facts she had collected without a focus to make meaningful connections or to develop a central point. "I had a topic but I didn't know what I wanted to do with it." The middle stage of the ISP, not the last stage, is time to begin to decide "what to do with the topic." Later studies of some of these same students in the workplace revealed that once students learned this process, they could adapt to a wide range of information-laden tasks. As one ISP case study participant explained, "The mind doesn't take everything and put it into order automatically and that's it. Understanding that is the biggest help" (Kuhlthau 2004, p. 77).

> ☐ *The middle stage of the ISP, not the last stage, is time to begin to decide "what to do with the topic."*

The Exploration stage of the ISP indicates an essential zone of intervention in Guided Inquiry to guide students with strategies and support for exploring ideas to identify an inquiry question in this early phase of learning when information and ideas don't fit together.

Formulation: Formulating a Focus

The task of the Formulation stage of the Information Search Process was to form a focus from the information found in the Exploration stage. Formulation of a focus marked the turning point of the ISP when feelings of uncertainty and confusion diminished and confidence increased. The kinds of information students were seeking also changed. Before students formed a focus, they explored general information on the topic. After they identified a focus, they gathered specific information about their focus. After they decided on a focus for their research, they emerged from a sense of confusion and feelings of doubt that they were on the right track to a sense of purpose and feelings of confidence in their ability to complete their task.

> ☐ *Formulation of a focus marked the turning point of the ISP when feelings of uncertainty and confusion diminished and confidence increased.*

Students who built background knowledge and identified ideas in the Exploration stage were prepared to form a focused perspective of the general topic. Students who did not form a focus continued to collect general information and experienced difficulty when they began to write and prepare to present their findings. By forming a focus, students identified an area of concentration, "something to center on," in which their ideas continued to grow and evolve based on the information they encountered in the Collection stage. This was the point when they could form a thesis statement if their assignment required one. The focus did not remain static but continued to take shape throughout the Collection stage. When the focus had been carefully formed through the Exploration stage, seeking a totally new focus was rarely

> ☐ *By forming a focus, students identified an area of concentration, "something to center on," in which their ideas continued to grow and evolve based on the information they encountered in the Collection stage.*

necessary. In forming a focus, students found it helpful to read over notes for themes and ideas and to reflect, discuss, and write about these ideas. Four criteria used to form a focus were: What is personally interesting? What is the requirement of the assignment? How much information is available? How much time do I have? (Kuhlthau 2004, p. 42; Kuhlthau 1994, p. 80). The Formulation stage of the ISP indicates a zone of intervention in Guided Inquiry to enable students to identify an important question from the interesting ideas they have explored to give direction for gathering information for deep personal learning. A well-developed, meaningful inquiry question is the focus for the inquiry process.

Collection: Collecting Information on Focus

In the Collection stage of the ISP, the task was to gather information pertaining to the focused topic. During this stage, the type of information that was sought shifted from what was relevant to the general topic to what was pertinent to the focus. A clear focus enabled students to discriminate between general information on the broad topic and specific information pertinent to their focus. A good focus could be adapted and altered while they collected information. Although students kept the focus clearly in mind, they also needed to refine and revise it as they read and took notes. The focus changed somewhat as information was gathered during this stage. When students expected change to take place, they actively sought to refine and adapt their focus through the information they collected. As students gathered information throughout this stage, they continued to learn about their focus. As they read, thoughts were more clearly defined and extended by new information. They took notes on the ideas and facts to build their understanding about the focus. Students who had difficulty collecting information frequently did not have a clear focus in mind. They lacked the structure upon which to build their ideas (Kuhlthau 2004, p. 104).

The Collection stage of the ISP provided strong evidence for the necessity of intervention in each phase of the inquiry process. It was important to note that forming a focus came at the midpoint of the ISP and was a critical turning point when interest in the project deepened as students got further along in collecting pertinent information about their focused topic. Guided Inquiry is based on the insight this research provides into a zone of intervention in the early phases for forming a meaningful inquiry question. At the Gather phase in Guided Inquiry, students have identified a clearly articulated inquiry question that provides direction for their gathering. Guided Inquiry is designed to involve students in the inquiry process from Open through Immerse, Explore, and Identify, but

❏ A clear focus enabled students to discriminate between general information on the broad topic and specific information pertinent to their focus. A good focus could be adapted and altered while they collected information.

❏ When students expected change to take place, they actively sought to refine and adapt their focus through the information they collected.

❏ Students who had difficulty collecting information frequently did not have a clear focus in mind.

❏ It was important to note that forming a focus came at the midpoint of the ISP and was a critical turning point when interest in the project deepened as students got further along in collecting pertinent information about their focused topic.

they aren't left to their own devices. Through Guided Inquiry they work in an inquiry community using a variety of resources, engaging in interesting ideas and collecting and learning from quality information. They build a body of knowledge, are introduced to numerous resources, and acquire strategies for gathering information. In the Gather phase students apply ideas, information, resources, and strategies to address the inquiry question. The ISP studies showed that students' interest increased along with a sense of confidence. This indicates a zone of intervention in Gather that enables students to locate, evaluate, and use detailed information to gain a deep understanding of their inquiry question.

Presentation: Preparing to Present

In the Presentation stage, the task was to complete the search and prepare to present the findings, usually as a written paper, sometimes accompanied by an oral or visual presentation or some combination of all of these. When students entered the last stage of the ISP, the main portion of their library research had been completed. Some students made a final survey to be sure they had not overlooked significant sources, to verify a citation of a source they had used, or to confirm a particular fact or idea. However, most searching was finished by this stage. Notes taken in the Collection stage were reread to identify main points around which to organize related information. In this way, students built a framework for presenting their findings about their focus of the topic. Students had a sense of relief after the search had been completed. However, the Presentation stage marked the beginning of the writing process that presented another set of challenges. Students who constructed their ideas as they collected information were well prepared for writing and presenting and often expressed a sense of accomplishment and satisfaction. Students who had not formed a focus, had rushed through their search, or for some other reason had not developed their thoughts through the ISP often felt disappointed at this point. Students who had not formed a clear focus in the ISP had difficulty writing their papers. A clear focus gave not only a frame for collecting information, it also provided a frame for organizing and writing the presentation. Writing blocks evident in the Presentation stage of the ISP show the importance of intervention for constructing learning throughout the inquiry process and the necessity for guidance in creating a way to share that learning with others. During this time, students gained a sense of ownership and of developing expertise (Kuhlthau 2004, p. 50).

The Presentation stage of the ISP indicates a zone of intervention for Guided Inquiry that enables students to create a way to share their learning. In the ISP the focus provides a lens to

❑ Presentation stage marked the beginning of the writing process that presented another set of challenges. Students who constructed their ideas as they collected information were well prepared for writing and presenting and often expressed a sense of accomplishment and satisfaction.

□ *Guided Inquiry separates this into two phases: Create and Share. Creating requires guidance for going beyond facts to interpreting meaning and to share what has been learned.*

□ *These feelings formed the basis for assessing what went well, what problems were encountered, and how to approach future research assignments.*

□ *In later studies, these same students referred to "my process" and the "way I learn."*

□ *Guided Inquiry is what the learning team does at each phase to guide students in the inquiry process to foster deep personal learning.*

organize thoughts for presenting. The ISP shows that students need guidance during this phase to make connections and interpret meaning for presenting their learning. Guided Inquiry separates this into two phases: Create and Share. Creating requires guidance for going beyond facts to interpreting meaning and to share what has been learned through a number of channels of communication and with a number of different audiences.

Assessment: Assessing the Process

In the ISP studies, students were asked to reflect on what they had accomplished after the assignment was completed. Most students felt quite satisfied with their progress. But some felt disappointed that their work had not met their expectations. These feelings formed the basis for assessing what went well, what problems were encountered, and how to approach future research assignments. Their reflection on what had taken place during the process and their expectations of the next time they encounter a similar task made them aware of their own search process. In later studies, these same students referred to "my process" and the "way I learn." Many also showed an inclination to continue to choose research topics in a similar area, building their expertise, with some even showing evidence of influencing career choices.

The ISP shows a zone of intervention for the Evaluate phase in Guided Inquiry that calls for reflecting on the whole process after everything has been completed. This time of reflection enables students to become aware of their own learning process and to see themselves as learning in phases. Guided Inquiry incorporates reflection for assessment throughout all phases of the inquiry process. However, evaluation at the close of the inquiry process is an essential component in Guided Inquiry.

The ISP research described what students experienced in the phases of the inquiry process. Guided Inquiry is what the learning team does at each phase to guide students in the inquiry process to foster deep personal learning. Guided Inquiry opens the process at Initiation, immerses in background knowledge at Selection, guides exploring interesting ideas at Exploration, guides identifying an inquiry question at Formulation, supports gathering to address the question at Collection, intervenes for creating and sharing at Preparation, and assesses and evaluates throughout the inquiry process (Figure 2.3).

The findings of these studies provide solid evidence on how to guide learning in the inquiry process and prepare students for learning, living, and working in the information age. The Guided Inquiry design framework is built around the stages of the ISP, and analysis of this research provides substantive direction for

Information Search Process and Guided Inquiry Design Framework

What students are doing in ISP	Stage of ISP	Phase of Guided Inquiry	What the inquiry community is doing in Guided Inquiry
Initiating the research project	Initiation	Open	• Invitation to inquiry • Open minds • Stimulate curiosity
Selecting a topic	Selection	Immerse	• Build background knowledge • Connect to content • Discover interesting ideas
Exploring information	Exploration	Explore	• Explore interesting ideas • Look around • Dip in
Formulating a focus	Formulation	Identify	• Pause and ponder • Identify inquiry question • Decide direction
Collecting information on focus and seeking meaning	Collection	Gather	• Gather important information • Go broad • Go deep
Preparing to present	Presentation	Create	• Reflect on learning • Go beyond facts to make meaning • Create to communicate
		Share	• Learn from each other • Share learning • Tell your story
Assessing the process	Assessment	Evaluate	• Evaluate achievement of learning goals • Reflect on content • Reflect on process

Figure 2.3 Information Search Process and the Design Framework

Guided Inquiry Design Framework	
Open	Invitation to inquiry Open minds Stimulate curiosity
Immerse	Build background knowledge Connect to content Discover interesting ideas
Explore	Explore interesting ideas Look around Dip in
Identify	Pause and ponder Identify inquiry question Decide direction
Gather	Gather important information Go broad Go deep
Create	Reflect on learning Go beyond facts to make meaning Create to communicate
Share	Learn from each other Share learning Tell your story
Evaluate	Evaluate achievement of learning goals Reflect on content Reflect on process

Figure 2.4 Guided Inquiry Design Framework

guiding and intervening in the inquiry process. The shape of the design framework follows the flow of confidence and interest of students in the inquiry process that will help you guide students through their learning (Figure 2.5).

Third Space: Where the Student's World Meets the Curriculum

Third space is the other area of research that has greatly influenced the development of the Guided Inquiry Design Framework. Where the ISP is the nuts and bolts of Guided Inquiry, third space is the underlying theme, the watermark of engaging students personally in their own school learning.

Third space is about creating a learning space where the student's world meets the curriculum. All too often school learning

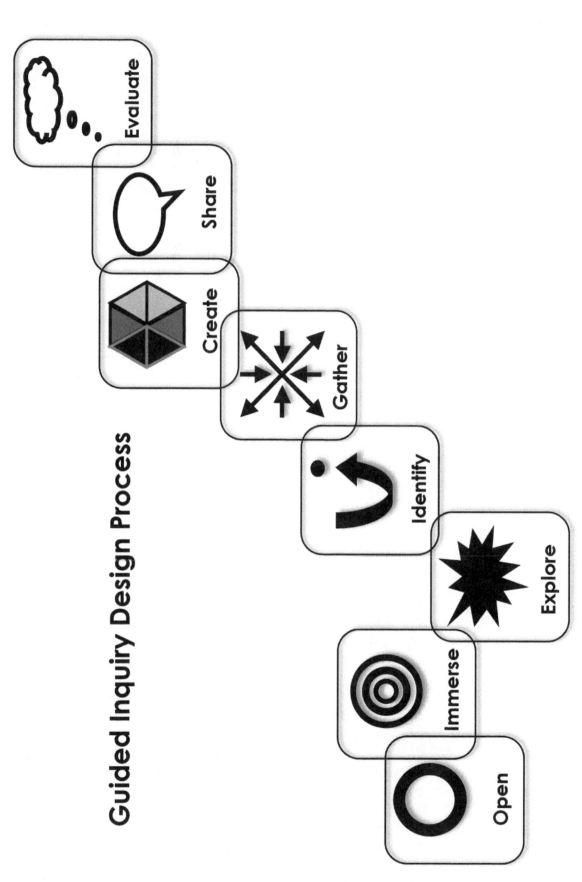

Figure 2.5 Guided Inquiry Design Process

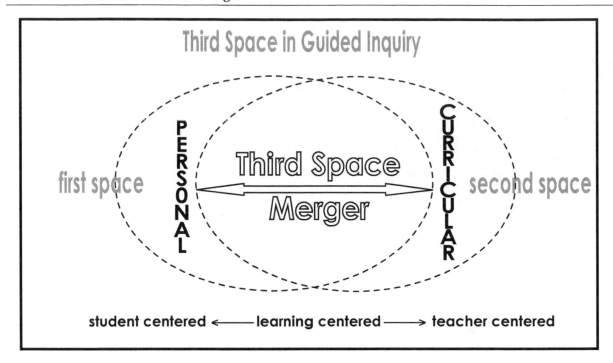

Figure 2.6 Third Space in Guided Inquiry

seems abstract or irrelevant and immaterial. The curriculum and the student's world need to be closely aligned for deep personal learning to take place. Continuity between the curriculum and the student's experiences outside the school promotes sustained, meaningful learning. In Guided Inquiry we use the concept of third space as the central theme for connecting to what is meaningful and important to the student throughout the inquiry process.

The students' world may be thought of as first space. It is the personal or cultural out-of-school knowledge and ways of knowing. Students have full lives outside of the school context and a wide range of information that they draw from to make sense of their world. Second space is the school's agenda, the school's curriculum. It is the official knowledge and the school's way of knowing. Often in schools the curriculum is the focus of learning, perhaps the only way. It is important for educators to help students use their cultural knowledge and experience from everyday life to help them understand curriculum content. A core tenant of social constructivist learning is that students construct their understandings out of what they know about their world.

☐ In the third space, students use their knowledge of the world to leverage the content of the curriculum into new understandings in their lives.

In the third space, students use their knowledge of the world to leverage the content of the curriculum into new understandings in their lives (Figure 2.6). Third space is when the first space of the students' world and the second space of the curriculum come together to make a third space where deep learning takes place.

Third space occurs when students' outside experiences are recognized as important and relevant to learning in school. Third space is when the students' experience and the curriculum overlap and merge to create dynamic learning.

The notion of third space arises out of the work of Bhabha (1994) who describes the third space as an "in-between" space where people draw upon language and cultural resources from many contexts to make meaning of the present world. When considered in the smaller school context, Maniotes (2005) calls for reconceptualizing classrooms to use outside-of-school knowledge to make sense of inside-of-school curriculum. Within this in-between learning space, students can construct new worldviews rather than be expected to take on the perspective of the school, teacher, or textbook. Although this type of learning space has been found to be difficult to achieve in classrooms, it is necessary for learning in the information age.

□ *Within this in-between learning space, students can construct new worldviews rather than be expected to take on the perspective of the school, teacher, or textbook.*

Guided Inquiry is designed to create a learning space where students' experience, taken from life outside school, is connected to curriculum content in meaningful ways. Maniotes (2005) identified conversational strategies that teachers can use to successfully nurture third space that are applied in each phase of Guided Inquiry. These strategies are questioning, modeling, listening, and encouraging.

□ *Guided Inquiry is designed to create a learning space where students' experience, taken from life outside school, is connected to curriculum content in meaningful ways.*

Third space often starts with a real question from the students. Wells (2000) explains that a real question is one that the teacher and students have a true desire to answer. Second, a real question is one that students could "take over and own" by offering opinions based on evidence from their own lived experiences as well as from the text. Real questions play into the context of classrooms by creating an organic environment for inquiry. Teachers and students come together to answer real questions because they honestly don't know the answer and want to learn what it is. As Gallas (1995) explained, setting an "I wonder" context helps children to get into a "let's find out mode." In other words, an inquiry stance opens questions to all members of the inquiry community. Questioning as a teaching strategy is a way to turn conversation back to students in order to redirect them and push their thinking to a higher level, in turn, opening the conversational floor to include more interactive dialogue. Guided Inquiry is anchored in this teaching strategy and most teacher talk comes in various forms of questions when guiding student learning.

□ *Third space often starts with a real question from the students.*

□ *An inquiry stance opens questions to all members of the inquiry community.*

The teacher models her own puzzlement and wonder to nurture questioning in the inquiry community. Modeling involves showing how rather than telling how; it involves describing what you are doing or thinking while you are demonstrating or in a

□ *Modeling involves showing how rather than telling how.*

follow-up debriefing session. As a conversational move, inquiry modeling also works to encourage students to bring in their own life experiences. Modeling is also an important part of the teacher's inquiry stance. Teachers model their own connections from outside that are relevant to the inquiry, helping students to know that they are expected to do the same. Modeling real questions for students is a good teaching strategy and at the same time nurtures third space.

Listening is actively, quietly engaging in students' conversations. Some active conversational moves show students that you hear what they are saying. These powerfully build third space through your actions. An inquiry stance includes purposeful interactions with students that give them messages, implicit and explicit, that you are interested in their ideas. Listening involves a response to students' comments that show you hear them. Listening includes acknowledging students' words while at the same time clarifying their meaning. Start with "Yes, so . . ." or "Oh, so . . ." beginnings, as in the following example:

☐ Listening involves a response to students' comments that show you hear them.

> **Student:** She said um. Opal asked if she did all um. Each thing in the bottle. And Gloria Dump said that um. I've done more.
>
> **Teacher:** Oh, so the bottles don't represent ALL the bad things she's done? Interesting. Anybody want to add to that?
>
> **Student:** I want to add! (Maniotes 2005)

In this example, the student was having a difficult time articulating his interpretation of events in the literature. Through the "Oh, so" construction, the teacher was able to reach down into the student's intention and articulate the essence of his idea and paraphrase it for the inquiry circle. Through this conversational move, the teacher showed she was listening and valued students' input. By ending her turn with an open question, the teacher opened the conversation back up to the group. The effect was that many students then wanted to add their own contributions. Repeating or paraphrasing students' ideas is a powerful listening strategy. Through active listening, teachers model good listening behaviors while at the same time show students that their ideas are important and essential to their learning.

☐ The teacher was able to reach down into the student's intention and articulate the essence of his idea and paraphrase it.

As Maybin (1999) warns, it is usually the teacher's voice that is highlighted through reformulation of thought (paraphrasing). Yet it was clearly the students' voices that were brought to the fore in the Maniotes study of third space. Instead of guiding their voices to imitate her own or to reflect the official space of the classroom as Maybin describes, the teacher's paraphrasing had a different effect. Her constructions emphasized the students' voices in the classroom because she took on an inquiry stance and built an inquiry community. This is what we seek to accomplish in Guided Inquiry.

Encouraging is another way to affirm students' responses and nurture third space. It is important to encourage students to bring personal knowledge into the school setting, because too often they are encouraged to only stay within the bounds of the text or the curriculum. Encouraging involves the creation of an accepting environment for sharing personal experiences that connect with curriculum learning in a meaningful way. Encouraging can be a subtle but important change in the way we talk. Small nuances of speech can have very different effects on conversation.

Teachers, often unknowingly, take on an evaluative tone that discourages student input. There are small ways of changing a simple sentence to make teacher comments less evaluative and more inclusive. For example, saying "huh?" or "is it?" at the end of a synthesis of a student's ideas can make a big difference. For example, look at these two in contrast:

- It's just not the right thing to do.
- Yea, it's just not the right thing to do, is it?

There is only a subtle difference between the two teacher comments. The first is a judgment. But the second example shows a teacher who makes a judgment and then throws it back to her students to ask them to decide what they think. This is part of what will be described in the coming chapters as taking on an "inquiry stance." Using techniques that open the conversation rather than closing it down is for inquiry learning and the inclusion of third space for learning. By using techniques and strategies that open conversations among students, third space becomes the norm rather than a rarity.

Guided Inquiry is anchored in the questioning teaching strategy. The Guided Inquiry Design Process creates a learning space where students are constantly calling on their personal knowledge to make sense of the most interesting information they are encountering in the inquiry process. The learning team guides students through the phases of Guided Inquiry toward third space by questioning, modeling, listening, and encouraging.

In each chapter on the design process is a section on how the learning team can model, listen, and encourage throughout the inquiry process. As you read these sections, think about engaging third space all across inquiry.

We mentioned in the beginning of this chapter that third space is a watermark of Guided Inquiry. A watermark is an image

□ Emphasized the students' voices in the classroom because she took on an inquiry stance and built an inquiry community.

□ Encouraging involves the creation of an accepting environment for sharing personal experiences that connect with curriculum learning in a meaningful way.

or pattern on paper that can be viewed in a different light. At a conference, an astute audience member and colleague told us that she saw third space as the watermark of Guided Inquiry. This is an apt metaphor because third space is ever present in Guided Inquiry Design, like a watermark is always on the paper. At times it is underground, at other times it comes to the fore. Some watermarks are obvious and others are hidden, only to be exposed by special light, but they are always present whether you notice them or not. Third space is ever present in Guided Inquiry, and the design framework helps us to nurture it throughout the phases of the inquiry process through questioning, modeling, listening, and encouraging our students' connections to the work.

□ *Third space is ever present in Guided Inquiry design, like a watermark is always on the paper.*

Research on ISP describes the personal experience of the process of learning from a variety of information sources. Learning is shown as a constructivist process that is commonly experienced by individual students. However, we are social beings. The inquiry process occurs in a social context. Schools are essentially communities of learners. School environments are ideal for inquiry when designed to consider the social outcomes of learning and scaffolding for social needs.

What's Next? Inquiry Tools

Through the creation of the Guided Inquiry Design Framework, tools for inquiry were designed and embedded within the process to make the best use of the social context for learning. These inquiry tools integrate strategies indicated by the research in this chapter that enable learning through an inquiry approach. The tools, when used regularly and throughout the process as designed, support social construction of knowledge and personal learning through inquiry. The next chapter defines each of these inquiry tools and explains the interdependence of the tools in the Guided Inquiry Design Framework.

Inquiry Tools:
Strategies for Guided Inquiry

The Information Search Process (ISP) research shows that inquiry learning is more than simply identifying a task, collecting information, and accomplishing the task. It is a complicated process of thinking and learning from a variety of sources that involves constructing a personal understanding. A close look at students in these studies revealed a number of ways they tried to work through the difficulties they had in the stages of the ISP. They talked to each other. They asked each other, what are you going to do? and what do you think about this? They *collaborated* and *conversed*. They wrote down ideas, made lists and short jottings, took detailed notes, and wrote extended papers. They *composed* all the way through the process. They kept lists of the sources that they planned to use. They *chose* sources that were useful and *chose* information to use within those sources. They outlined their ideas. They organized their ideas in an outline-type *chart*. They worked on their project over several weeks. They *continued* to work until the project was completed.

The Six Cs

These strategies were developed into the six Cs for intervening in students' ISP (Kuhlthau, 2004) to help them work through each stage of learning from a variety of sources (Figure 3.1). Intervention strategies based on the six Cs apply a constructivist approach to learning that enables students to build their own understandings. Here the inquiry tools are introduced as a structure for successful implementation of the six Cs across the inquiry process.

Intervention Strategies for Guided Inquiry	
The Six Cs	
Collaborate	Work jointly with others.
Converse	Talk about ideas for clarity and further questions.
Compose	Write all the way along, not just at the end; keep journals.
Choose	Select what is interesting and pertinent.
Chart	Visualize ideas using pictures, timelines, and graphic organizers.
Continue	Develop understanding over a period of time.

Figure 3.1 Intervention Strategies for Guided Inquiry: The Six Cs

Collaborate

Inquiry occurs within a social context. Collaboration enables students to try out ideas and hear other perspectives at various phases in the inquiry process. The ISP studies showed that students struggle when they treat inquiry as an isolated competitive undertaking rather than as a cooperative venture. Students often find that consulting with classmates enables them to learn from each other. In Guided Inquiry, students collaborate in large groups called inquiry communities and in small groups called inquiry circles. Collaboration diminishes the experience of isolation in inquiry and enables students to co-construct during the process of learning.

Converse

Conversation helps students to articulate their thoughts and identify gaps and inconsistencies in their thinking. In Guided Inquiry, conversation is an intervention strategy to help students work through the stages of the inquiry process. Conversations in inquiry communities and inquiry circles enable students to talk and raise questions about the facts and ideas they are encountering. Conversation is essential for the social construction of meaning. In the early stages, conversing opens up possibilities for interesting ideas to investigate. During the Exploring stage, conversation enables students to express their feelings of confusion and uncertainty and to receive support and advice on how to proceed, which leads to identifying a meaningful inquiry question. In the Gathering stage, conversation centers on interpreting the meaning of the information and facts students are collecting about the inquiry question.

Compose

Composing is another strategy that promotes thinking throughout the inquiry process. Composing enables the construction of new ideas and shapes learning. Writing in inquiry journals is an important strategy to foster thinking and reflecting in each stage of the inquiry process. Guided Inquiry introduces journals in the early stages for recording interests, feelings, and impressions, and the use of journals continues into the later phases of summarizing, interpreting, and learning. Composing is an essential strategy for forming thoughts and developing understanding in the inquiry process.

Choose

Choosing enables students to learn how to take control of their own inquiry process. In Guided Inquiry, the learning team helps students to see choosing as a creative strategy in learning. Students are guided to make choices and select what they find interesting, important, and pertinent in order to address their inquiry question. Good choices are those that lead students to generate their own understandings rather than thoughtlessly copying and reproducing text. Locating, evaluating, and using quality sources involve making yes, maybe, and no decisions throughout the inquiry process and recording choices in inquiry logs.

Chart

Charting enables students to present a large amount of information in a compact way. Visualizing is a way of constructing that enhances the learning process. The very act of charting enables thinking about many disparate ideas. Concept maps and graphic organizers are excellent tools for connecting and organizing ideas. Timelines and flowcharts are useful for demonstrating various phases of the inquiry process and the sequence of sources used, as well as the ideas that are emerging. Drawing is a form of charting that young children use to express ideas. Inquiry charts are valuable tools for making connections between the many ideas that emerge through the inquiry process to come up with an inquiry question and a central theme.

Continue

Continuing involves the sustained attention of staying with a project to completion. It requires persistence and perseverance. The ISP studies showed that the best motivation for continuing was driven by personal interest in a focused perspective that developed over the course of the inquiry process. Guided Inquiry encourages students to come to well-formed, meaningful questions that are personally interesting and provide natural, intrinsic incentives for continuing. Continuing leads to becoming an expert for the inquiry community and being able to share learning with others. By continuing, students experience a successfully completed extensive project that fosters an understanding of how to learn in a complex information environment. Longitudinal ISP studies showed that these experiences are often remembered and valued by students as among the most important learning experiences from their school years.

Inquiry Tools: Implementing Strategies

The six Cs are gradually introduced and integrated into the phases of the inquiry process through inquiry tools (Figure 3.2): students collaborate and converse in inquiry communities and inquiry circles; compose in inquiry journals; choose in inquiry logs; and chart in inquiry charts. These tools are designed so that students are practicing strategies for inquiry across the entire inquiry process. They are learning ways to manage their inquiry, develop their thinking, and learn from a variety of information sources. These inquiry tools help students engage in the six Cs for learning throughout the inquiry process.

Building an Inquiry Community: Collaborate and Converse as a Community

Schools are places where people come together in communities to learn. The school is the larger inquiry community in which individual classes exist. Each class is its own inquiry community within this larger school community context. Building an inquiry community prepares students for inquiry learning and is a task that is critical to the success of Guided Inquiry in your school. In Guided Inquiry, students take full advantage of working in a community of learners called an inquiry community. Their inquiry community surrounds and supports them in their inquiry learning.

In the inquiry community, inquiry habits of mind, dispositions in action, and constructivist beliefs about learning are core values represented in each individual's actions within the community. Other common community values and beliefs are that inquiry is relevant to learning in life, learning happens in a social context, collaboration enables individual capacity, personal connections are essential, and reflection is a critical component of learning.

Inquiry Tools: Embedded Strategies for Inquiry	
Inquiry communities for collaborating	An inquiry community is a collaborative environment where students learn with each other in a large group.
Inquiry circles for conversing	Inquiry circles are small groups organized for conversations about interesting ideas, meaningful questions, and emerging insights.
Inquiry journals for composing	Inquiry journals provide a way for individuals to compose and reflect throughout the inquiry process.
Inquiry logs for choosing	Inquiry logs provide a way of keeping track of the quality sources that are chosen as important for addressing an inquiry question.
Inquiry charts for charting	Inquiry charts provide a way to visualize, organize, and synthesize ideas in the inquiry process.
Inquiry tools for continuing	All of the inquiry tools are for continuing and sustaining the inquiry process to completion.

Figure 3.2 Definition of Inquiry Tools

In an inquiry community, students learn with each other in a collaborative environment. Collaboration enables students to raise questions, hear other perspectives, try out ideas, and share their own views at various phases in the inquiry process. Students find that consulting with classmates enables them to clarify their ideas and learn from each other. Inquiry communities provide opportunities for semistructured sessions for asking questions, brainstorming, sharing, reflecting, presenting ideas, and learning. This is accomplished through a combination of whole class conversations and small group interactive work. Collaboration is an important component in constructing new knowledge and building deep understandings. The teaching team sets a tone for collaborating that is open and accepting, as well as intellectually engaging.

An Inquiry Stance

Building the inquiry community with students will take time. An inquiry community is made up of students with an inquiry mind set. An inquiry mind set enables students to ask meaningful questions and take on an inquiry stance. Prior to opening the inquiry unit, the community begins to form by structured experiences and instruction on critical thinking, listening, conversing about ideas, and looking for evidence, as they collaborate to learn together and ask meaningful questions. These structured experiences in the classroom and the library build an accepting environment for learning from each other with mutual respect for each other's ideas.

There are many ways to grow an inquiry community and develop an inquiry stance. Each community of learners must come together and establish community routines and values that center on the inquiry process. An example of building an inquiry stance using images can be found in the work of Visual Thinking Strategies (VTS; http://www.vtshome.org/) developed by Visual Understanding in Education (VUE). VTS was developed as a way to help students develop and recognize visual literacy by looking at art works and discussing the meaning and the evidence of that meaning in small groups. The main questions asked in VTS are: What is happening? What do you see that makes you say that? What more? Students are guided to answer the prompt, give evidence for their ideas, listen to each other respectfully, and discuss rationally any idea that might have more than one correct answer. VTS is more about developing observation and drawing conclusions based on evidence, that is, critical thinking skills rather than questions. VTS helps students develop the habit of mind of listening to each other, collaborating, and conversing about ideas.

Learning to Ask Meaningful Questions

An inquiry stance is based on being able to ask meaningful questions. Students can gradually learn how to draw real questions from the texts they are reading and viewing. Through knowledge of asking real questions, students can learn how to analyze texts, make decisions about importance, and justify their ideas. Asking real questions lays the foundation for building an inquiry community.

In one intermediate classroom, the inquiry community gradually developed as students learned to ask real questions. This was not something the children naturally knew how to do on their own. Questioning was a main focus of the teacher from the start of the year, as she taught her students to ask more and more sophisticated questions about texts.

The students gradually became aware of how questions could help them make meaning from their readings. The teacher explained, "At the beginning of this (year) kids were writing things down, but they weren't questions. By the time we got to it in November, they were really good at it. . . . It was definitely a process."

This transition came about because the teacher and the literacy specialist planned a study of questioning for September and October. The teacher scaffolded the students' learning until they gradually took on a larger notion of how questions could help them to think deeply about the texts they were reading. The teacher described the process as follows:

In the beginning we opened it up as a free for all for questioning. "I'm going to read . . . and you're going to ask any question that comes to your mind." The questions were, "How old was that boy?" "What color were his shoes?" They were asking things that they already knew the answers to or that didn't matter. So then we went back and started to say, "Go back and mark the questions that are going to help you understand the story." That took a couple of times, definitely to realize. "I don't have to know what color his eyes are to understand the story." Things like, "That's not going to help change how I think about the story."

The teacher and the literacy specialist helped the children analyze their own questions in order to eliminate unnecessary questions and dig deeper into what would make a difference for comprehension and interpretation. It took some time to get the students to stop asking questions that they already knew the answers to.

The teacher explained how the inquiry community worked through this together to create an understanding of better questions. She said, "We had them go back and analyze their own questioning . . . sharing it out with their friends and saying, 'Is this going to really help you understand the story better?' The students rated the questions and then chose the burning question or ultimate question that they still have that just wouldn't leave their minds. They got them to think of questions that get students thinking beyond the book or into their own life. And that kind of leads them to connections in other things as well" (Maniotes 2005).

In Guided Inquiry, teachers and librarians work together in learning teams to design ways to build an inquiry community with their students. For instance, they collaborate to identify texts and other sources that would be good choices for students to practice questioning skills. Then, they design inquiry sessions during both class and library time when students can work on these sources. Next, they model questioning when they think aloud about these texts to show their own analysis and demonstrate their own inquiry stance. Then, they have their students ask their own questions about texts, fiction and nonfiction, and video that take them beyond the facts into their own lives.

It's important to emphasize questions that lead to comprehending, interpreting, understanding, and learning together in an inquiry community. By scaffolding experiences, it's possible to gradually reveal how questions can draw meaning from a text and lead to further inquiry. A collaborative inquiry community made up of students with an inquiry stance is fertile ground for Guided Inquiry.

Inquiry Circles: Collaborate and Converse in Small Groups

Small groups organized in inquiry circles are an essential feature of Guided Inquiry. Inquiry circles can be adapted to students of all ages from early elementary through high school. An inquiry circle consists of four to six students arranged around the topics of the inquiry for conversing and collaborating to construct an understanding.

Inquiry circles provide a platform for conversations about ideas that students are encountering in a variety of sources. They create a space for students to talk about ideas that are meaningful to them, raise questions that they are curious about, and help each other to construct meaning. The discussion of third space in Chapter 2 provides an example of these kinds of conversations in inquiry circles.

Inquiry circles change across the inquiry process. The learning team organizes students into inquiry circles by the end of the Immerse phase when the students have enough background information to select an initial area of interest. These groups will continue to meet regularly and as needed for the duration of the inquiry process. Conversations in inquiry circles provide support for each student's developing ideas and evolving concerns in each phase of the inquiry process. The goal of the inquiry circle is to have a high level of conversation with all participants. During these conversations, students are expected to collaboratively construct understandings with a give and take of ideas.

At times, inquiry circles are informal settings for students to collaborate and converse about their inquiry journal or inquiry log entries and how the process is going. At other times the learning team may find that the students need structure to accomplish the level of conversation required. The team can assign jobs to the students so that they can engage in a meaningful conversation for each phase in the inquiry process and move the inquiry forward. The learning team needs to tailor jobs to students' needs and what they are striving to accomplish in the inquiry process, always keeping in mind the overall learning goals of the inquiry unit.

For example, the learning team decides that the students need more structure to engage in a deep, meaningful conversation. Jobs are then designed to help students know how to prepare for an intellectual conversation. The jobs also help scaffold the conversation around sources and the topic. The goal is to teach the students the kinds of things good researchers do when they take part in a collaborative conversation and are prepared to interact as a research team.

Each inquiry circle member completes one job at a time for one round until they know how to do each job. Then they are required to do all of these things in preparation for an inquiry circle meeting. These jobs become habits of mind and are routinized to help them prepare and participate in conversations in inquiry circles. The work prior to the inquiry circle meeting prepares the students for the conversation; over time, students learn that preparation makes for a more useful conversation.

The jobs designed for one group during the Explore phase are described here. These jobs help the students dip in to read a common text that would lead them to co-constructing background knowledge and identifying a meaningful inquiry question. The jobs include the following:

- **Questioner:** asks questions about the texts.
- **Note Taker:** reads to find interesting facts and ideas to bring to the group.
- **Connector:** reads to make connections between texts and real life, as well as what they know about the topic.
- **Messenger:** reads the piece to discern author's purpose.
- **My Take:** reads and asks questions to report their own ideas and reactions.
- **Listener:** reads and highlights important sections in the text and takes a larger role during the conversation to summarize and identify important ideas and questions from the group.

Inquiry circles also foster social skills. Each member is dependent on the others and each is responsible to the others. When the students work together in small collaborative groups, it helps ease the uncertain feelings that arise when each student works in isolation. Inquiry circles help students develop an understanding of the big picture and encourage interesting ideas as they emerge. As small groups of students continue to work together throughout an inquiry process, they develop respect for different skills and types of learners and come to understand and rely on each other's strengths.

Students are interacting, cooperating, and collaborating in the inquiry process under the guidance of the learning team. The role of the learning team during inquiry circle meetings is to rove and monitor and guide where needed, but not to hover. The students should increasingly take responsibility for the conversation, the work, and the outcome of the meetings.

It's ideal to have an even number of students in an inquiry circle so that it is easy to facilitate different groupings. Idea-sharing in different contexts and sizes of groups is important. Sharing in pairs offers an exchange that helps to clarify and articulate thinking because the students can spend more time engaging in conversation.

Wikis and blogs can provide a useful structure for the documentation of the work in and around inquiry circles. Some of the benefits are that students have easy access to the groups work at all times. The learning team can follow the work and track the development across the inquiry and assess progress.

Inquiry Journal: Compose Throughout the Inquiry Process

Inquiry journals are a tool for individual composing and reflection. The journal documents the whole inquiry process and captures the holistic experience that each student can return to and learn from. Without the inquiry journal, the valuable documentation of the personal inquiry journey is lost. Inquiry journals can be adapted to students of all ages from early elementary through high school. Time is set aside for each student to compose in order to construct understandings and reflect on learning. For the youngest learners, the inquiry journal includes labeled drawings with a sentence or two. As students increase their capacity to compose, the journal follows the inquiry process and changes to match the work of each phase as they construct deeper understanding. It also includes reflection on the inquiry process to help students become aware of their own learning.

The inquiry journal is a routine embedded into the design of Guided Inquiry to help students think and reflect. It builds the habit of mind of reflection necessary for learning through inquiry. Capturing an idea in the inquiry journal frees up cognitive space for linking multiple thoughts together, building on an idea, or moving on to create new ideas.

A journal can take any form. A fully implemented Guided Inquiry approach for 21st century learning is possible from a low-tech setting to the most up-to-date format. For example, an inquiry journal can be a simple pencil paper composition book, a word processing document, one laptop or device per child, or it can be housed on-line as a wiki, blog, googledoc, etc. There are many web 2.0 tools, including social bookmarking and note-taking tools (Evernote, etc.), that can be used to document and track students' progress. At the end of the process, students take all entries and look at what they have and see what connections can be made. This is an organizational challenge. Page numbers, and dates on pages can help to retain the sequence of paper journals. Color coding and Post-its can help with tracking ideas and themes. Journals in digital format may present other challenges when students want to look back and synthesize all the information within the process. Although it is easy to search digital format for terms and keywords, a word cloud (wordle.net) can be used to analyze the texts at a word level. However, the question remains, how do we know what to search for? A survey of all the information can help students see the themes and connections in the information.

It is important to remember that the form the journal takes is not as important as the role it plays in the inquiry process. The inquiry journal is the place for students to reflect on their learning, examine their thoughts and feelings, and write about all of these at each phase in the process.

The inquiry journal can be open ended or more structured and can take on different formats depending upon the task and learning needs. Journal entries often are not complete thoughts, and the journal must be a place where students feel comfortable adding their own personal connections and wonderings. Entries should include personal musings; various levels of thinking, drawings, and diagrams; and sophisticated complete ideas. The accumulated journal entries will be an uneven writing sample. In addition to students' free writing entries, inquiry journals include prompts from the learning team for directed composing. Prompts include quick writes; reflections on the process; answers to a question at a key moment; assessments at the beginning, middle, and end of the process; and other formats that are provided throughout this book.

The ISP studies showed that it is important to monitor students' thoughts, feelings, and actions during the inquiry process. By the evolving nature of the process, inquiry journals are "time-sensitive materials." They provide a window into the students learning and sometimes show the learning team when a student needs guidance and a learning opportunity arises. This is called the zone of intervention. The learning team can skim inquiry journals for learning opportunities revealed in students' thought processes represented in their journals.

Inquiry journals act as a self-assessment tool for students at the end of the inquiry process. Students use this record of the inquiry to reflect on how and what they learned. Conferences with students around the journal focus conversations on individual learning obstacles and progress.

Individual guidance is needed in this kind of learning, and the inquiry journal keeps the team abreast of students' needs so that they can intervene when students need assistance to move on. It's likely that every student will need guidance at some point during the inquiry process, and the journal is one way for the team to keep alerted to those individual struggles. Data from the inquiry journals also help the team designate groups of students with a similar learning need for instruction and guidance.

Inquiry journals are introduced in Immerse and used throughout the inquiry process. Over the course of the process, the entries change. Students list interesting ideas in the Immerse phase and jot down thoughts that lead to meaningful questions as they dip in and read during the Explore phase. They also can reflect on the process by considering their thoughts, feelings, and actions as they change as indicated by the ISP. Inquiry journal entries become longer and more detailed and reflect pertinent information to the inquiry question as students go deep in the Gather phase. In the Create phase, students include charts and syntheses as they pull ideas together and return to earlier entries to highlight quotes and paraphrasings to cite in their final presentation.

Inquiry Log: Choose and Continue

Choosing enables students to learn how to take control of their own inquiry process. In Guided Inquiry, students learn that inquiry requires choices: choosing what to pursue, choosing what is of value, choosing what to leave out, choosing what is enough. Good choices are those that lead to deep understanding rather than thoughtless copying and reproducing texts.

The inquiry log is not simply a record of sources. When a student decides to add a source to the log, a choice has been made. The inquiry log is a record of the active, evolving choices of usefulness that a student makes in the Explore and Gather phases of the inquiry process. The inquiry log is subtitled, "Making Choices and Tracking the Journey," so this purpose is clear to the students. The inquiry log was designed for students to efficiently monitor their choices and for the learning team to easily check on students' progress. It is a practical tool that tracks students' learning and progression through the inquiry process.

Some choices are more important than others for formulating the inquiry question and shaping the inquiry. In the Explore phase, choices lead to forming a meaningful question and establishing the direction and extent of the inquiry. In the Gather phase, the inquiry question provides a frame of reference for choosing what is most useful and what is less useful. Guidance by the learning team enables students to apply choosing as a creative strategy for pursuing interesting ideas through the inquiry process that deepens their knowledge and understanding

Inquiry logs are introduced in Explore and used again in Gather for students to keep a record of their choices. In Explore, before students have identified their inquiry questions, the logs are used for recording interesting sources that students come across. Most of the choices in Explore fall into the "may be useful" category. Students' inquiry logs include citations of the sources they have located with notation of why the source may be useful. Sometimes students identify sources they think may be useful at one point, and then find them not to be useful later on and discard them in the end. Everything on the inquiry log is not always used or cited in the final product.

In Gather, students make choices of sources that are useful and pertinent to the inquiry question. When students go deep, they are guided to choose a few of the most useful sources to concentrate on. Students return to the inquiry log and document where they go deep. The inquiry log reflects this choice when students check "use it." Keeping a log in this way tracks the journey of the student in the inquiry process.

Ethical use of information is essential for students to learn in all phases of the inquiry process. The inquiry log is an important tool for acknowledging the originator of a work, whether it's an author, expert, or an originator of an idea. Students need guidance to learn to give credit where credit is due when they tell their story with another's ideas. They learn to cite sources of all types in all modes and formats. The record of full citations should be in the format recommended by your school. A simple citation is used by young children, and a more advanced format is introduced to upper elementary and middle school students. It is important that students form the habit of acknowledging an author's work in their early encounters with inquiry.

Inquiry Charts: Chart and Choose

Guided Inquiry uses inquiry charts as a creative strategy to help students visualize ideas, issues, questions, conflicts, and connections that emerge during the inquiry process. Inquiry charts enable students to accomplish many things. Charting helps students to display large amounts of information. Students are able to pull together many disparate ideas to identify questions and find themes. It is an act of construction that enhances learning.

Inquiry charts take a variety of formats, from very informal jottings to intricate flowcharts and webs. With guidance, students can get into the habit of using inquiry charts to help them think through difficult points in the inquiry process. Less formal charting may be used for thinking through questions and sharing ideas. Simply taking a piece of paper and quickly drafting an idea is helpful in the early stages of inquiry. More formal charting in the form of developing patterns to connect ideas such as a web or map are helpful in the later phases of the inquiry process.

A variety of shapes and configurations can be applied. Large circles may represent big ideas, with smaller circles representing subordinate ideas with connecting lines and arrows. Stick figures, various shapes, and colors may be used. Inquiry charts can show patterns of similarities as well as anomalies of things that don't fit. Inquiry charts provide opportunities to be creative, opening up a range of possibilities for students to visualize their ideas and questions. Students of all ages can benefit from visualizing their thoughts through inquiry charts.

In the Identify phase, inquiry charts are valuable tools for thinking about the many ideas found through Explore to identify an inquiry question. In the Create phase, inquiry charts help students make connections among ideas and information they have gathered to prepare to interpret and share their learning in a meaningful way. Although inquiry charts are recommended specifically for Identify and Create, they are useful tools for mapping ideas at any point in the inquiry process.

Readingquest.org (http://www.readingquest.org/strat/) has resources for charting from a social studies perspective. Thinking maps (http://www.thinkingmaps.com/) is another source for types of charts and how to use them. More graphic organizers can be found http://www .eduplace.com/graphicorganizer/ and http://www2.scholastic.com/browse/article.jsp?id=2983.

Inquiry Tools are Interdependent

Inquiry tools are used together and interdependently (Figure 3.3). Many interactions happen throughout inquiry and these tools support the interactions. All interactions occur within the context of the larger inquiry community. Students use the tools to practice the six Cs and apply them to learning for deeper understanding. Inquiry tools are the means and structures for students to learn and for the learning team to guide and assess the learning.

Conversing in inquiry circles helps students to construct knowledge, build connections between sources, and relate to the ideas of peers. Some conversations in inquiry circles are brought to the larger group and inform the entire inquiry community.

The inquiry journal is a central tool for Guided Inquiry. The journal is where ideas are generated from simple notions and evolve into complex thoughts. Inquiry charts are created out of the content of the journals. Inquiry logs are a record of the sources and choices that are written about and expanded upon in the journal. Charts and logs can be housed in the journal, so that all documents are together. Ideas developed in inquiry journals can be brought to the inquiry community and used to inform the conversations in inquiry circles. When inquiry circles include

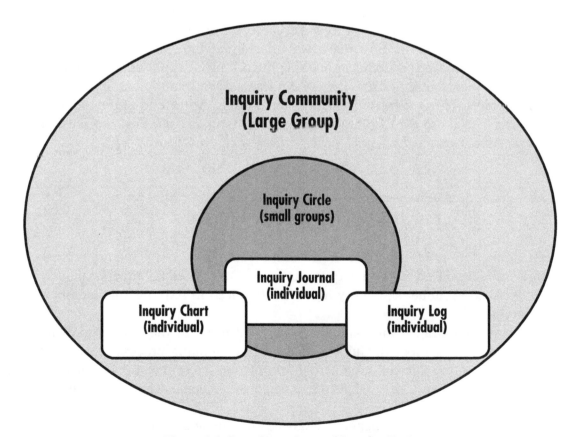

Figure 3.3 Interdependence of Inquiry Tools

jobs, the work is prepared in the journal and brought to the circle meeting. The inquiry log is a record of locating, evaluating, and choosing sources. Students use the log to document the sources they will use and decide on a core of the most useful sources. In the Gather phase, the inquiry journal is a companion tool for choosing information within sources. Students choose what to quote and what to paraphrase. In Share, students use charts to explain their learning to others in the inquiry community. In Evaluate, all tools are reflected upon in students' self-assessment of the process and content of learning.

Inquiry Tools for Assessment and Evaluation

Assessment is an active process throughout Guided Inquiry for both students and the team. Continual reflection and assessment throughout the inquiry process reveal what students have learned, when students need intervention, and what intervention is required. Learning team members plan assessment of inquiry collaboratively and work to assess the different aspects of the process. They work individually and together to assess the various types of learning that occur through inquiry. Student grades should also be tied to the ongoing assessments rather than just to the final project. The tools are used as regular check-ins and assessments. By providing time to reflect on the use of tools, the inquiry process becomes more transparent for students and allows them to develop an understanding of how to manage their own learning.

Each phase of the inquiry process offers an opportunity to sift through the tools as an assessment point. For example, inquiry journals provide the learning team with a record of evolving learning from each student. It is a useful record for the learning team that documents all aspects of inquiry learning. It can be a way to examine thoughts, feelings, and actions so that the learning team can track student learning in each phase of the inquiry process. Inquiry journals, inquiry logs, inquiry charts, inquiry circles, and work in the inquiry community provide the data points for assessment throughout the process. At the end of the inquiry, the team comes together to evaluate the learning by using all the tools as data. This is discussed in depth in Chapter 11, Evaluate.

Inquiry Tools: Across the Guided Inquiry Process

Each inquiry tool is introduced in one of the first four phases of the inquiry process. Inquiry communities are introduced at Open; inquiry circles are introduced at Immerse; inquiry journals also are introduced at Immerse; inquiry logs are introduced in Explore; and inquiry charts are introduced at Identify.

The intervention strategy of continuing is applied in all of the inquiry tools throughout all phases of the inquiry process. Guided Inquiry is a continuing process of raising curiosity, exploring ideas, forming questions, gathering information, and reflecting on meaning over an extended period of time in order to construct a personal understanding from a variety of information sources.

Guided Inquiry supports students with advice and guidance that continues throughout all phases of the inquiry process as they apply all of the inquiry tools: inquiry communities, inquiry circles, inquiry journals, inquiry logs, and inquiry charts. The inquiry tools provide a structure for managing the inquiry process that enables students to develop patience, persistence, concentration, and sustained attention for deep learning.

What's Next? Open

The inquiry tools are an integral part of the Guided Inquiry Design Process. The following chapters describe in detail how the tools are strategically integrated into each phase of the inquiry process. Included is a section for each tool employed in that phase as well as many examples for use. The next chapter is Open, the first phase of Guided Inquiry.

Open

- **Invitation to inquiry**
- **Open minds**
- **Stimulate curiosity**

4

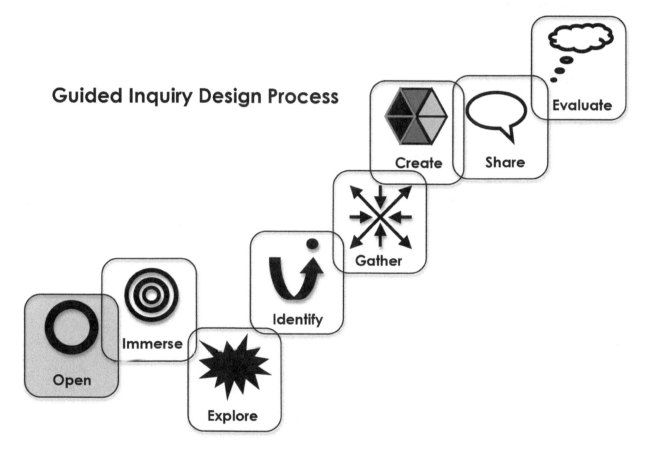

Guided Inquiry Design Process

Open · Immerse · Explore · Identify · Gather · Create · Share · Evaluate

Open is the invitation to inquiry, the beginning of the inquiry process. Open is a distinct and important phase of the process that sets the tone and direction of the inquiry. Once the learning team has decided on the learning goals, they create a powerful opener that invites the learners in, establishes an inquiry stance and introduces the general topic to engage the inquiry community.

The main challenge is to open students' minds and stimulate their curiosity. The open session inspires students to want to pursue the inquiry. The opener is designed to spark conversations about ideas and themes, pose questions and problems, and highlight concepts related to the subject. These conversations stimulate students to think about the overall content of the inquiry and connect with what they already know from their experience and personal knowledge.

The Research

Initiation Stage of the Information Search Process

In the initiation stage of the Information Search Process (ISP), the teacher announced a research assignment that requires information from a variety of sources to be accomplished over a number of weeks. The task of students in the first stage is to think about a topic for research. Students often feel apprehensive and uncertain about what is expected of them and overwhelmed at the amount of work ahead. Talking with other classmates about requirements is a natural action to take, but some feel they should be "going it alone" and that checking with others might not be "entirely fair."

Instead of starting with the assignment, the research indicated that Guided Inquiry required a different approach. That is why the design of the Open in Guided Inquiry works to open the conversation, ensuring that students understand that it is not only fair to talk about their ideas and questions, it is necessary to have these conversations at this phase. The design indicates that the assignment is not introduced until after students arrive at a meaningful question to pursue in the Identify phase.

In Open, the learning team develops an inquiry community that forms an environment for the inquiry process. Rather than announcing a research assignment, Guided Inquiry opens with big ideas and overarching themes that open minds and capture attention. Opening draws students in to think about what they already know, care about, and are curious to know more about. In Guided Inquiry, the only "going it alone" is when students connect the topic to their personal interest.

Too often, without giving too much thought, an inquiry project is announced and students are expected to come up with a topic or a question and jump right in. But the research on the ISP shows that this is a confusing time when students need guidance in thinking about the subject and strategies for getting started.

Open in Guided Inquiry

The learning team opens with an invitation to inquiry. Open is where the investigation begins for the inquiry community. The team sets an invitational tone with a short but powerful learning event, that is, an opener that sparks students' interest and elicits prior knowledge.

The Open phase provides a "hook" that catches students' attention and opens their minds to the inquiry. A short dramatic video is an excellent way to spark curiosity. Something as simple as an object, photograph, or art image can provide the stimulus to help students begin to think about a subject. Without this stimulus, it may be difficult to access prior knowledge. For instance, if a class is beginning a study of water, simply asking, what do you know about water?, might elicit blank stares. The question is too general.

Contrast that with the following. If you held up a bottle of drinking water, the conversation would open up and could be guided toward particular learning goals. For example, if the big idea is "Water in Our Lives," then the team would guide the conversation about where water comes from, how we use it each day, why we put it in bottles and buy it, and when we get it from the tap. When designing Open, the team chooses a large theme for the inquiry and identifies an essential question that is relevant to the content and connects to the students' lives.

The opener will depend upon your learning goals. A photograph from *National Geographic* magazine of people carrying water from a well (*National Geographic* Magazine, April 2010, http://ngm.nationalgeographic.com/2010/04/water-slaves/johnson-photography) would evoke different questions about water use around the world. In a different approach, use of artwork such as Boys in a Dory (http://americanart.si.edu/collections/search/artwork/?id=73938), a Winslow Homer painting at the Smithsonian American Art Museum of boys sitting in a boat by the ocean, might get the community talking about how humans interact with the ocean for recreation, as a food source, and as a source of income or livelihood. The learning team should design an opening session that will lead students to ask questions and generate ideas about a subject.

The learning team must carefully consider what will engage this particular group of students at this point in time. This is why each inquiry is different, even if the learning team is implementing plans that they have taught previously. Each inquiry community is unique. Learners come to the process with different life experiences, habits of mind, skills, and interests. The learning team must be flexible enough to make changes if students seem more interested in a different aspect of the inquiry than students in previous years or if students seem to have less or more understanding of the subject.

Openers emphasize the ideas that engage student interest and connect with their world, offering an invitation to begin the inquiry process. When learning is the focus, it is critical to set the tone that the *ideas* are paramount. The learning team recognizes that the end product will be a reflection of the ideas that are generated.

Invite Learners In

The Open phase provides the foundation for successful learning throughout the inquiry process. It is a way to invite the students into the exploration. By drawing links to students' lives, we invite them to examine curriculum content in ways that have meaning to them. So, a common question is, how can I be sure that the inquiry is something students are fascinated by and care about? When designing Open, the learning team is mindful of arriving at the third space to create the learning-centered community. The team considers the following questions: How can we gain students' interest and curiosity? How can we change their attention from "What does the teacher want me to do?" to "Why is this important to me?" or "How is it relevant to my life?" Moving from a teacher-centered environment to a learning-centered environment is a primary design concern of the Guided Inquiry process.

A successful opening enables students to connect to the content of the curriculum in ways that are important to them and have meaning for them. An Opening that invites students into a learning space where the curriculum and their world meet fosters understanding. There is more to creating this learning space than drawing out what is familiar. Students consider relevance as they ask, Why is this topic, question, or theme worth studying? How does the inquiry fit into my world? Why is it important? What is personally compelling about the inquiry? Why does it matter?

Excellent openers provide a platform for these types of questions to arise and be reflected upon by students. They include conversations around these questions in the inquiry community. They build shared background within the group, providing the rationale for why to proceed and what to pursue.

Establish an Inquiry Stance

The learning team guides opening by assuming an inquiry stance that is open to what students bring to the group from their lives. Following is an example of how a teacher turned a difference of opinions into an opportunity to investigate at the opening of inquiry: In an opening discussion about the Apollo missions to the moon, the teacher asked, "What have you observed about the moon?" One student claimed, "You can see the moon only in the night." A few others disagreed, "NO! You can see it in the day too!" The teacher knows the "answer" to this disagreement and at this point has a choice to make. The teacher could have said, "No! You can see the moon in the night and the day." This would have the effect of squelching the inquiry altogether. But instead, she said, "Hmmm . . . we have two differing opinions about this. Let's think about this together!"

This is choosing an inquiry stance. Using an inquiry stance facilitates students' peer-to-peer interactions and increases inquisitiveness in the inquiry community. Whether it is a group of younger students or high school students, a nonjudgmental and accepting attitude guides students to construct their own understandings. The objective at opening is not to answer the questions that are raised but to create an inquiry tone that will extend outward into essential, meaningful questions for inquiry. Being conscious to maintain an inquiry stance is important throughout Guided Inquiry, especially when setting up the learning experience in the opening.

Engage the Community

Openers work to rally the students around a topic, and build excitement as they engage the whole inquiry community in an idea or theme. One third grade teacher found a new way to open her unit on electricity that captured the hearts and minds of her students.

The class gathered for science time and the teacher got them up out of their seats into a large circle on the carpeted area. She had them hold hands and held up a small pink ball. When she held it up, the class was silent; it was nothing out of the ordinary, just a pink bouncy ball. Next, she had the girl to her right hold it with her. The ball lit up and buzzed! The students were astonished and thrilled when the ball buzzed again as the electricity circulated through every member of the class as they held hands and closed the circuit.

This quick opener made the students wonder and got them to pose their own real questions about electricity. It highlighted the concept of circuits and their workings because students realized that the electricity could go through their bodies. It also opened up a conversation about the hows and whys of this light-up ball and electricity in general. It brought electricity home for the students and set the inquiry in motion.

The science demonstration and ensuing conversation provided this class with a rich opening that engaged the community and made them want to investigate more. Openers pique students' interest and bring a community of learners together around a topic.

The first stage of the ISP, Initiation, described students' experiences at the beginning of a typical research project. At the beginning of an assignment, the teachers' instructions frequently were centered on the mechanics of the project. Teachers focused on logistical considerations such as how many sources were required, what was the length of the final project, and other details about the format (font, number of pages). Soon after the teacher announced an extensive research assignment, the students were expected to select a general topic right away. Students weren't ready to do this. They felt apprehensive over the unfamiliarity of the subject content, uncertain about what was expected of them, anxious about the work ahead, and confused about ways to get started.

One caution at this point is to avoid focusing on the mechanics of the project and on the end product too early in the process. When a teacher's instruction centers on the grading rubric at a project's initiation, the students follow that example and also focus too much on the product, format, and how they will be graded. This takes their attention away from the ideas that lead them into inquiry. For instance, if a teacher announces at the outset that students will be creating a PowerPoint presentation on the Hispanic experience in Denver at the beginning of the 20th century, the students are likely to concentrate on the mechanics of creating a PowerPoint. Rather, this is a time when the students should connect with the content and ideas. Mechanics and logistics can be attended to later in the Gather and Create phases of the inquiry process.

Provide adequate time for students to build background knowledge and engage in interesting ideas. Without adequate background knowledge, students are not ready to ask meaningful inquiry questions. Often a well-meaning teacher provides a list of defined topics at this point. Giving students a list of questions or topics to choose from doesn't provide the foundation for constructing their own learning in the inquiry process. Because these are the teacher's questions, not the students', using this kind of list can cause problems further on in the inquiry process.

What is the Team Doing?

The learning team uses modeling, listening, and encouraging to foster third space in inquiry learning. In the Open phase, it is important to start by modeling an inquiry stance. The team is listening to students' questions, gaining an understanding of students' background knowledge, and encouraging questioning and having an inquiry stance.

Modeling

During Open, the team's role is to model an inquiry stance of questioning, being open to all responses. The team also models their own connections from life to the inquiry topic so that the students feel comfortable expressing their ideas.

Listening

The team is listening for good ideas and questions that draw out what students know and are interested in, leading to possibilities for further inquiry. They are listening for connections and misconceptions that surface right away.

Encouraging

The team encourages student interaction and openness in an accepting environment for an inquiry community. They also encourage students to make connections from their outside lives to the ideas presented in the opener. They encourage questioning, divergent thinking, opposing viewpoints, and an inquiry stance.

What is the Learner Doing?

During Open, the students use the inquiry community as a forum for conversation and collaboration. A safe environment is built as ideas give rise to curiosities in the opening phase.

Collaborating and Conversing

During Open, students are conversing in their inquiry community before constructing their initial thoughts and understandings about the topic. Talking about new ideas, raising questions, and listening to the ideas of others occurs naturally in active inquiry communities. In Guided Inquiry, a comfortable yet challenging atmosphere is an essential characteristic of an inquiry community. Conversation calls upon students to express their thoughts about what they know that is sparked by the opener. Conversing helps them to think through the new ideas that have stimulated their curiosity. Conversation that leads to learning occurs in a safe environment where students know that they can try out ideas and change their minds. Conversing and collaborating in the inquiry community are ideal strategies to draw students into the Open phase and in turn the entire inquiry process.

Ideas for Open Sessions

Because each inquiry is tailored to the learning needs and knowledge of the community, the possibilities are endless (Figure 4.1). The team has a variety of expertise from which to draw as they design the opening experience. It introduces the theme and includes a meaningful, essential question that is relevant to students' lives.

In one team's design conversation, the team was ready to design a powerful opener for an inquiry into careers for middle school students. They first thought that each member of the team should dress up in character representing a different career. In that role, they would answer students' questions about the kind of work the job entailed. When they thought together a little longer and reflected on the possibilities, one member had a discovery. She called it an "epiphany."

EXAMPLE SESSION PLAN

OPEN - IMMERSE - EXPLORE - IDENTIFY - GATHER - CREATE- SHARE - EVALUATE

Learning Goals: Invitation to inquiry, open minds, stimulate curiosity
Location: Classroom
Team: Learning team
Inquiry Unit: Water in Our Lives

This Open session uses object-based learning to get students thinking about water in our lives using an unopened water bottle.

Starter Time: 10 minutes Inquiry community	Gather children for a whole group session (inquiry community). Hold up a water bottle. Start discussion by asking, "Why do we put water in bottles and buy it from the store?" List responses, modeling ways to record discussion in small groups during work time. Display these questions for the whole group to think about and open the inquiry stance by encouraging a short discussion on each: • Where does water come from? • Where do you get your water? • When do you use water? • For what purposes? • How much water do you think you use every day? • What if you didn't have water?
Worktime Time: 20 minutes Inquiry circles	Organize students in inquiry circles (you may want to do this ahead of time) to discuss these questions and record responses on a note catcher.
Reflection Time: 15 minutes Inquiry community	Group share: Have students take one really interesting idea from their conversations in the inquiry circle to share with the whole group. At close of the session, have children think about what they want to know more about. The following questions my help spur their ideas: • What do you wonder about water? • What surprised you? • What connections did you make to your life? Process closure: Ask students to reflect on the following question in their journal or as an exit card for the session: How did the water bottle help you to get thinking?
Notes:	Immerse session following this session: A visit to a water storage tower or water treatment plant. Objects work well as openers. They get students thinking about the essential theme of inquiry and how it relates to them. Many different kinds of objects can be used to catch attention and stimulate curiosity.

Figure 4.1 Open Example Session Plan

The speech teacher suggested that they bring an object, such as a store-bought burrito or a GPS device, and have the students think about where it came from. The essential question was still evolving but included how many different people it took to get a specific object into the students' hands and the jobs that those people had.

The team realized that this second opener was the better of the two ideas because they knew the design features they wanted in a solid opener. It would start from what the students know and expand outward in ways that they couldn't predict in the planning. It was centered in the curriculum they had to teach but opened up the third space and included actual students lives into the conversation. They saw the rich potential this had for getting kids to think beyond the here and now and to think about the origins of a familiar object. This opener had the power to get students really thinking and questioning careers in a whole new way.

An object can provide a powerful connection as an opener. Objects make links to the past, for example, sharing a toy from World War II era. Objects from the past can tell much about the people who owned them; their values; and the time, place, and even economic conditions of the time. Objects can open inquiries on a wide variety of topics and can work to generate questions and help students wonder and get into the inquiry mood about the topic of study.

Openers include all kinds of different experiences and resources. Objects such as museum artifacts, realia, unusual objects, and everyday objects can draw students into a problem for inquiry. Museum artifacts or reproductions of artifacts can connect students to the past in concrete ways. Realia, such as a ticket to the Worlds Fair or a train ticket from a different time period, can act as a type of story starter that makes the time, place, and people come alive. An unusual object can come from another culture or time period and serve as a puzzle. The students can use the unusual object to problem-solve and figure out how the object was made or how it is used. An object such as a toy or a shoe made from a recycled tire could say a great deal about the values and resourcefulness of the people who made it. Students can think about different design solutions to common human problems around the world, such as how to obtain and carry clean water for everyday use.

Articles and blogs with thought-provoking messages can get students thinking about different sides of an issue. Literature, such as poems, short essays, and picture books with a strong concept, can help students relate to a particular time, place, or subject.

Primary sources, such as photographs, documents, and diaries available at a local historical society or courthouse as well as on the Internet on the Library of Congress American Memory site, offer a contrast or comparison with the students' own lives to get them thinking and talking about ideas. Like historical objects, these sources can bring history to life and allow students to imagine what the real people who lived long ago felt or thought about issues of their day.

Visual art, photographs, paintings, models, and sculpture can provide a unique perspective on the humanities. The artwork gives a window into ideas that the artist grappled with and that may have historical or personal interest for the students. Art can be a very good opener for an inquiry unit that deals with personal identity and expression.

When location is important, maps can provide a way in. Maps offer a visual reference for geographical issues that people face, such as barriers created by physical and political boundaries. Maps from the past can be contrasted with maps from the present to show change over time. Science experiments and science demonstrations of all types can be powerful for starting inquiry when used to open an area of investigation.

Students are connected to video today, and short videos with a powerful message, such as TED talks (www.ted.com), or concept films with a short, punchy message grab students' attention. Thought-provoking podcasts on specific subjects or controversial topics like the ones produced by Radiolab (www.radiolab.org) can work like literature to provide a thought-provoking atmosphere around a topic and still appeal to the auditory learners. Music recordings that connect to a time, place, or concept can be used to set the inquiry tone and invite learners in. There are endless possibilities for openers that accomplish the goal of opening minds and stimulating curiosity to get the inquiry off to an interesting start.

Take time when designing openings to ask around, look around and be creative. The extended team can be tapped to help the core team brainstorm ideas. Collaborations like the one described above can be powerful and offer something that one person thinking alone would never get to. That is the synergy of the team at work. When the entire team works on the design of the inquiry process from the beginning to the end, the collaborative team's effect on learning impacts the community in rich and meaningful ways right from the start.

What's Next? Immerse

After Open, the inquiry community needs additional background knowledge to define the general subject and scope of the inquiry. Students cannot be expected to develop a meaningful question for inquiry directly after the Open phase. Although they have been asking questions in their inquiry community, students will need substantial background knowledge about the subject before they are ready to develop a productive inquiry question. In the next phase, students immerse in the content of the inquiry as they build subject knowledge and continue to connect to their interests and curiosities.

Immerse

- **Build background knowledge**
- **Connect to content**
- **Discover interesting ideas**

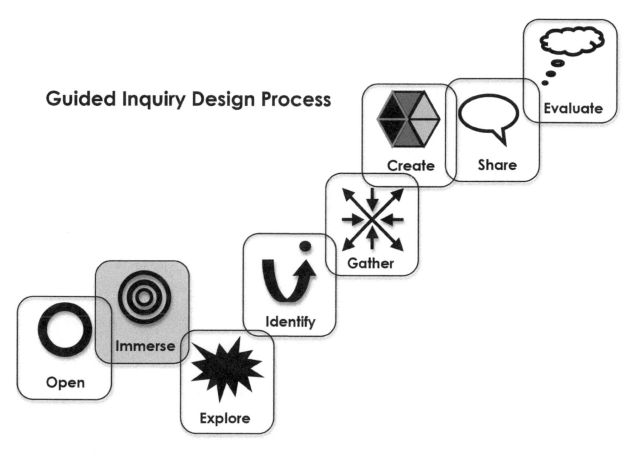

Guided Inquiry Design Process

In the Immerse phase, the inquiry community builds background knowledge together through an immersion experience. The learning team designs engaging ways for students to immerse in the overall ideas of the content area under study. For example, the inquiry community can read a book, story, or article; view a video; or visit a museum.

The main task of Immerse is to guide students to connect with the content and to discover interesting ideas to explore further. Learners are guided to think about what they already know and what seems particularly interesting, curious, surprising, or troubling. As they build background knowledge, students reflect on ideas that matter to them and are worth further investigation.

The Research

Selection Stage of the Information Search Process

In the Selection stage of the Information Search Process (ISP), students selected their research topic within the subject area of the assignment. Before students selected a general topic, they were confused and somewhat anxious. After they made their choice, they often experienced a brief sense of elation, followed by apprehension at the extent of the task ahead. Feelings were quite evident in the Selection stage of the ISP. Some students wanted to select a topic quickly and dive right in to collect information and complete their research. The Selection stage involved a zone of intervention that was not being met. Students often selected topics with little background knowledge. Although they felt relieved, even briefly elated, they were not prepared for the difficulties ahead when they settled on a topic.

In a similar way, many inquiry approaches start by requiring students to come up with an inquiry question. A typical inquiry project begins with a brainstorming session to elicit questions from the class. Then each student chooses one of the questions to investigate. There needs to be lots of groundwork before students can form meaningful questions that they really want to pursue and are actually worth investigating.

Immerse in Guided Inquiry

Immerse connects all of the students in the inquiry community with the big picture of the curriculum content area of the inquiry. It provides an overview that sparks ideas but doesn't overwhelm or bore with too much detail. In this phase, the whole group experiences a shared orientation in preparation to beginning their search for information about interesting ideas in the Explore phase.

 Caution must be taken to ensure that immersion experiences provide just the right amount of information for the beginning of inquiry. If too many facts are delivered at once or too many sources introduced, students become overwhelmed. When students appear bored, it is often because they are being hit with too much detail before they are ready to comprehend it. The immersion experience should not be loaded with disparate, specific facts to commit to memory but should serve as an overview of background knowledge to build upon.

A careful balance is necessary to learning. The learning team designs Immerse sessions that engage students to immerse in background information and overall ideas of the content area under study. Immerse enables all of the students to get a general picture of the content of the inquiry and to build common background knowledge. Immersion experiences are designed to accomplish broad learning goals by connecting students to the content of the inquiry, building background knowledge, and discovering interesting ideas.

There are a variety of ways an learning team can design immersing experiences depending upon the time and content under study. Immerse can be a single session or can take more time depending on students' knowledge, students' age, and the complexity of the topic. Some curriculum topics are much more complex than others and require a more in-depth immersion experience. Younger learners may not go deeply into the content of a topic. Students with little background knowledge will need different immersion experiences than those with more experience and advanced subject knowledge. The learning team needs to take all of these considerations into account in planning the length and depth of immersing experiences for a particular group of students.

Immerse should connect students to the content under study in personal ways in the third space. The learning team designs immersing experiences that are engaging and personally connect to their specific group of students. What works for one group of students may not work for another group. Immerse needs to be tailored to the students' interests, abilities, and needs in order to inspire them to engage their own interests. The individual nature of Guided Inquiry is what makes it an effective way of learning but also a challenging way of teaching.

Students have been organized in an inquiry community for some time and are accustomed to working together. They are ready to participate in immersing sessions within their inquiry community. Immerse can begin with an experience within the inquiry community that gives an interesting broad picture and motivates students to want to know more. This is followed by a conversation in inquiry circles about the ideas that emerged from the experience and a time of reflection in inquiry journals about the meaning of the ideas. An immersion experience provides lots of interesting information to stimulate students thinking rather than specific facts that they are expected to commit to memory. Immerse is designed to provide an overall picture and include interesting ideas that inspire students to want to explore information in order to learn more.

The following sections include examples of the use of videos, literature, and museums to immerse students in background knowledge with the intention of drawing out interesting ideas to explore in the next phase of the inquiry process. In each of these examples, the team uses a variety of ways to build knowledge, connect content, and experience and discover interesting ideas.

Build Background Knowledge

Immerse is designed to guide students to build a common base of background knowledge. Not all immersion experiences take extensive time. For example, young children can build background knowledge in a single Immerse session. Early elementary students studying shadows and light begin by watching one part of an episode of the PBS television show *Sid the Science Kid* in which Sid begins to wonder about what shadows are and how they can be made (Sid the Science Kid, Episodes, Shadow Investigation http://www.pbs.org/teachers/sid/activities/light/). During the program, Sid explores shadows in many different ways that suggest possibilities for the students to try themselves. The students learned what a shadow is, how a shadow is created, and the situations that need to be in place for shadows to occur. From the short video clip they had enough information about shadows to begin to wonder more about them.

After watching the program, students became interested in finding their own shadows on the playground, using flashlights to create shadows in the classroom, and creating shadow boxes and shadow puppet theaters to explore shadows and how they work. As the team designs time to immerse in shadow play after the video segment, students interact with shadows and come to understand them in new and personal ways. This particular group went on to explore shadows for a full month through active engagement, fiction and nonfiction text, and in different media. The rich immersing experience laid the groundwork for a fertile, in-depth learning experience about shadows.

Older students may take the time to get a quick look into the resources available on the inquiry topic. A preliminary search is an initial check into information to get a sense of what's there. They can check to see if there is a lot of information, some information, or no information on the topic or theme. From their preliminary search, students begin to build a base by choosing a general reference to build some background knowledge. Students today tend to go directly to wikipedia.com for a general reference point. The learning team can provide other options such as an online encyclopedia for quick, general reference. A preliminary search gives a feel for the content or an overview of the important aspects related to the topic, such as who, what, when, and where, that lead to interesting ideas to explore.

Connect to Content

As the Common Core Standards state, "At a curricular or instructional level, within and across grade levels, texts need to be selected around topics or themes that generate knowledge and allow students to study these topics or themes in depth" (p. 58). Many times the literature is carefully chosen for interpretation in a language arts class; however, once the text is completed, the unit is over.

When we use the Guided Inquiry Design Framework and place the literature toward the beginning of the study, the learning from and about the text extends outward into content. Through an inquiry following a common reading, students apply their understanding from the reading and conversation about the text. By reading a common piece of literature, they have generated some core knowledge around the topic from which to explore more deeply and later to identify an inquiry question. Literature is useful for connecting students to a time period through quality historical fiction, where the characters come alive in the setting as students interact with the text.

In one example, a social studies/history teacher teams up with the language arts teacher and school librarian to examine the theme "American Grit." This specialized team is able to connect students in the content. They offer expertise in both disciplines and provide a literary lens, as well as a historical lens, to the reading. The learning team designs sessions that immerse students in the content by reading a quality piece of literature, such as *The Grapes of Wrath* (Steinbeck 1939). Through the reading of the text and subsequent conversations, the students immerse into the time period and confront some of the important issues of people who lived during the Great Depression. Students gain a core understanding of the Depression era from a variety of perspectives on which to build and a wealth of interesting ideas to explore.

Historical fiction, such as *Bud not Buddy* (Curtis 1999), can be used with younger children to immerse in the same time period (Kuhlthau, Maniotes, Caspari 2007, p. 65). Literature provides students with opportunities to identify with characters and connect personally to the events and story of a time period. The Common Core Standards suggest a list of resources for each grade level that provide students with a range of complex, high-quality readings (pp. 32, 58). These types of texts fit well within the Immerse phase of inquiry.

Immersion in literature with the group as a whole inquiry community is combined with conversation in inquiry circles. Experiences that immerse the inquiry community are followed by conversations in inquiry circles to go deeper into personal meaning. The inquiry circle provides a structure for small group conversations to facilitate thinking about the immersion experience. While in the Immerse phase, students can discuss and then list the interesting ideas or issues that arose from the story that may be worth further investigation and lead to inquiry questions.

Discover Interesting Ideas

Museum exhibitions or museum-based programs are excellent ways to immerse students in a topic and find ideas that are interesting to them as well as being academically relevant. Museum exhibitions are usually designed to explore various issues surrounding a particular theme or subject and are designed for the type of informal or free choice learning that you want to provide in an immersing experience. Museum programs are more structured experiences that lead learners to a desired learning goal or goals.

When designing museum exhibitions into the inquiry, the learning team can consult with museum educators and even add them as extended team members. Together, they design a learning experience around the visit to immerse students in the topic. This meeting may happen in person, on the phone, through Skype, or via email. Inclusion of the museum educator in this planning ensures a cohesive match between learning goals and resources.

Museum programs, which are available at museums around the United States and world, are inspiring beginnings to inquiry learning when designed as an immersion experience. Historical societies and historic houses often have traveling trunks with costumes and replica objects from a particular time period. Natural history museums, science centers, and zoos may have a teaching collection of shells, minerals, fossils, or other natural objects to lend to schools. Many museums also have online exhibitions with images, primary source documents, explanatory text, and interactive programs based on exhibitions or objects in their collection. These kinds of collections can augment what is already available in the school library. The school librarian on the team is an expert at finding resources and can assemble all sorts of materials from within the school library and the world beyond the school to enrich the immersing experience.

What is lacking in these programs and cannot be supplied in a program kit developed outside of the inquiry community is the personalization that happens when the inquiry continues past immersion. The learning team guides the understandings that emerge from the immersion experience into a complete inquiry to address a meaningful question.

Bridge Basics is an example of a program for immersing upper elementary or middle school students in design and engineering issues. The program, developed by the National Building Museum (www.nbm.org), began as a museum program and then was developed into a classroom kit, which is available to those who cannot visit the museum (http://www.nbm.org/assets/pdfs/youth-education/bridges_erpacket.pdf).

The packet provides information, primary source materials, and activities for students to learn what bridges are, different types of bridges, and historical and geographic information about bridges in Washington, D.C., and around the United States. Over several different sessions, students are immersed in understanding the design choices involved in building, including structure, environment, economic, aesthetic, and historic considerations. This immersion experience builds extensive background knowledge on what engineers think about when designing each type of bridge. Students work in inquiry circles to learn about each type of bridge and beam, arch, truss, and suspension and to find out why they might be used at a particular geographical site. At the end of this immersion, each inquiry circle uses recycled materials to build a model of a different type of bridge.

The learning team decides what is important and interesting about this information for their students at this time. Perhaps a bridge or tunnel is being proposed in the vicinity and there is a debate about what type of bridge should be built. Perhaps the information could be applied to another engineering or design problem in their neighborhood or city or state. What more do the students want to know and what can they do with this information? How can they generalize from this experience and apply the information, knowledge, and skills developed to a new situation or topic? This is where Guided Inquiry and the learning team are critical for turning good activities into deep, lasting inquiry learning. It is at this point that the learning team observes the inquiry community to notice what ideas are emerging that could form the inquiry circles for the remainder of the inquiry process.

What is the Team Doing?

The learning team uses modeling, listening, and encouraging to foster third space in inquiry learning. In the Immerse phase, it is important to cultivate the inquiry stance through modeling, listening to students' connections, and encouraging students' input and questioning.

Modeling

During Immerse, the learning team continues to model the inquiry stance by accepting many different perspectives, incomplete ideas, and speculations. It is the team's role to gather that information without closing down students by offering conclusive or judgmental responses. The team supports learning by gathering information on what students know about the subject. At this point, it is useful to model and give permission to speculate. For example saying, "I've heard somewhere that . . . ," "I think that . . . ," "I wonder if . . . ," " It might be . . . ," is very different from "I know that. . . ." Speculation at this point leads to deeper thinking. The team supports third space and encourages students to bring in connections from their experiences and their lives to the conversation. When teachers model their own thinking, questioning, and connecting, students come to know that this is the expectation for their thinking, questioning, and connecting to draw out their own interesting ideas.

Listening

The learning team is listening for personal connections and interesting ideas that come to the surface. The team is listening for speculations as well as some forms of expertise. For instance, a student may have traveled to a specific region and have some experience that relates to the topic. They may have something in their family background or culture that could add a unique perspective.

Encouraging

There is a certain amount of risk involved in sharing information and opinions about your experience and knowledge. The team positively encourages all voices and provides a supportive and safe environment.

What is the Learner Doing?

During Immerse, the students use tools to converse and compose in order to connect to the content of the new inquiry. Students gather in small groups to engage in conversation in inquiry circles. They also reflect on their own connections, questions, thoughts, and ideas as they compose in inquiry journals.

Organize Inquiry Circles: Learning in Small Groups

Students are actively involved in inquiry circles in the Immerse sessions. Students' conversations in inquiry circles during Immerse provide support for their developing ideas and emerging questions. The learning team organizes students into inquiry circles, typically composed of four to six students. Inquiry circles are tailored to your students' needs and abilities, the curriculum content, and the inquiry process, keeping in mind the overall learning goals.

At Immerse, inquiry circles are flexible groupings. They may not solidify until students identify their inquiry question. For example, one group may work together in Immerse, but an entirely different group may form at the Identify phase once students are more certain of the direction of their inquiry.

Students may be arranged by subtopics that are related to the content under study, as described in the bridge unit example in this chapter. In that unit, students were grouped with a particular task in mind that helped them understand common concepts around bridge design. In this case, the learning team groups the students.

At other times, the team may let students form their own inquiry circles based on their interest in a particular aspect of the study. Whenever possible, it is important to provide opportunities for students to find their own interests and connections to the material. Connecting to content is a learning goal of Immerse, and having students choose their inquiry circle based on their interesting ideas works toward their progress in immersion. This doesn't mean that anything goes. The curriculum provides the content theme and lens with which to guide students' choices. Interesting ideas need to be generated with clear learning goals in mind that are connected to curriculum standards. When students generate interesting ideas, it is essential that the learning team take time to ensure that there are clear curriculum connections to the larger theme.

Choice in inquiry circles highlights the difference between planning an inquiry and designing an inquiry. In planning, every piece is thought through prior to the task. When we design, we take an open inquiry stance to the learning that will unfold. When designing inquiry, we provide time and opportunities to immerse in the larger theme in order to build background knowledge. The importance lies in the immersion into the content to stimulate interesting ideas. Designing an inquiry using the Guided Inquiry Framework helps learning teams stay focused on these important components of the Immerse phase, rather than getting bogged down in the details of planning activities. Design forces the team to rise above the activity level of planning to see the big learning picture. Decisions around inquiry circles, grouping students, building background knowledge, drawing out interesting ideas are grounded in the goals of this phase of the inquiry process and set within the larger frame of the inquiry and learning.

Inquiry Journals for Composing

Learners use inquiry journals to express their thoughts, feelings, and actions across the inquiry process and compose to reflect on every aspect of the content. During Immerse, students use the inquiry journal to jot down interesting ideas that surface in the immersion sessions. Students may begin their inquiry journals by writing about what most interests them. As they write about the immersing experience, they make connections to what they care about. They build upon with what they already know as they begin to construct new understanding. The learning team responds with comments in students' journals that guide them in selecting intellectually engaging ideas to pursue.

Composing promotes thinking throughout the inquiry process. The purpose of the inquiry journal changes as the inquiry progresses. The inquiry journal is started with early thoughts and feelings when the inquiry process begins. In Immerse, students write about the interesting ideas they learn in the immersing experience and that come from conversations about the experience with other students in their inquiry circles.

In one class, students were asked to complete "exit cards" in their inquiry journal after the immersing experience. At the close of each session, students were given time to reflect on their thoughts. This helped introduce students to the idea of the journal, prepare the way for deeper responses that would follow later in the inquiry process, and generate interesting ideas out of their immersion experience. These Immerse journal entries were short, inviting writing exercises. Sometimes they took the form of a "free write" for five minutes at the end of a session. Other times they were asked to write their thoughts, feelings, and actions. This was useful for students to generate thoughts and make them aware of what they only partially knew. These entries also provided the learning team with the information needed to assess where students were connecting to content, generate interesting ideas, and be aware of their actions. The exit card journal entries helped the team keep a pulse on the learners as they went through this phase of the process. When students were not progressing, the team quickly intervened by conferring with those students in the next session to guide them in a more productive direction. Figure 5.1 shows examples of journal entries for the Immersion phase that prompts for these two types of exit card writing.

In the Immerse sessions, the three inquiry tools for building strategies in inquiry are beginning to take shape. The team has now established an inquiry community and continues to facilitate the development of the community to immerse in a mutual experience. Students are working in inquiry circles to get multiple perspectives on what other students know and to think about the topic and draw out their own interesting ideas to pursue. The inquiry journal is introduced as a means to compose and personalize background knowledge, inform meaningful conversations about content, and reflect on interesting ideas.

INQUIRY JOURNAL PROMPTS

Inquiry Journal Prompts	Interesting Ideas to Explore
Write three things you learned in today's session.	I learned that . . .
Write about something that surprised you or was new to you.	I was surprised that . . .
Write something that you already knew about. Tell how you know.	I knew that ...
List some ideas that seem interesting to you.	Interesting ideas I have are ...
List ideas that you want to know more about.	I would like to know more about ...

Figure 5.1 Inquiry Journal Prompts

Ideas for Immerse Sessions

Immerse sessions can take place in the classroom or school library media center or they may be excursions to community resources (Figures 5.2 and 5.3). The Immerse sessions should help students to build the background knowledge needed to ask good questions about the topic. At this point, the inquiry community reflects on the general overview information together as a way to discover the most interesting and important ideas for the group to pursue.

These session plans are meant to help you think about the Immerse phase in detail. The session plans in Figures 5.2 and 5.3 provide a model of the many appropriate activities that help build students' background knowledge in the Immerse phase. The example session plan comes out of a real inquiry unit and shows the details of one session in that phase.

Students read the same piece of literature and discuss how it relates to the inquiry topic and draw out interesting ideas for further investigation. Historical or science fiction, nonfictional texts such as essays or speeches, or fantasy fiction are all good choices. The Common Core Standards include a list of speeches and letters for grades 6 through 12, such as Letter on Thomas Jefferson by John Adams, Farewell Address by George Washington, Letter from Birmingham Jail by Martin Luther King, Jr., and Common Sense by Thomas Paine, that make excellent choices for immersions. The important factor in choosing texts for the immersion experience is that it be appropriate reading material for the students' level and that it be tied to the curriculum topic by theme, time period, or setting. For younger students, this may be accomplished through read-aloud or read-along sessions. For older students, the reading may be done in or out of class with discussions in inquiry circles.

Students may watch a play, movie, or video as an immersion into the inquiry topic. The media event may be fictional or nonfiction. Informational videos or documentaries are excellent ways to immerse students in an overview of the content. There are many educational podcasts that can also serve as immersion experiences. After listening or viewing, the students form into inquiry circles to discuss what was most surprising, troubling, or inspiring about the piece. The students uncover ideas and connections that pique their curiosity.

There may be a museum or community resource that can provide a unique Immerse session that will engage students. A museum exhibit can often provide an engaging, multimedia presentation of the major themes or chronology of a particular subject. As with any source, it is important to understand that an expert in the field who has a particular point of view about a subject organizes museum exhibitions. It can be interesting to view two exhibitions that present opposing viewpoints on one subject or historical era.

Depending on the inquiry subject, there may be a community resource, business partner, or experience that would serve as a field excursion for immersion into the inquiry. The learning team may also choose to create a virtual tour of several carefully chosen Internet sites for the students to browse in order to better understand the topic and build background knowledge.

What's Next? Exploring

Immerse builds background knowledge and grounds learners in connections between the content and their lives. Students come out of the immersion experience with a host of interesting ideas that are worth exploring further. In Explore, students build on the background knowledge they acquired in the Immerse phase to explore the ideas they have chosen as personally interesting in preparation for developing meaningful inquiry questions.

MODEL SESSION PLAN

OPEN - **IMMERSE** - EXPLORE - IDENTIFY - GATHER - CREATE- SHARE - EVALUATE

Learning Goals: Build background knowledge through a shared experience to prepare for more in-depth questioning in Explore.
Location: Museum, library, or theater
Team: Learning team and extended team member

This Immerse session plan provides an example of using a museum, videos, and books to help students build background knowledge and draw out general concepts and interesting ideas without becoming overwhelmed or bogged down in too much detail.

Starter Inquiry community Inquiry journal	Converse in the Inquiry Community: Refer to the Open Session. What ideas arose during the reflection in the Open Session that were most intriguing? What do you wonder about the ideas? How can we find out more? Compose Inquiry Journal: Have students draw a sketch, write a list, or write short notes reflecting on the Open session. Write what is personally interesting to them in their inquiry journals.
Worktime Inquiry circle	Have students work in small groups-inquiry circles-as they immerse in content and build background knowledge together. Immersing in content can take on a variety of forms including an immersion experience. Visit a museum exhibition, see a theatrical performance, watch a video, read a work of fiction such as a short story, poem, or novel, or read a work of nonfiction such as an essay that relates to the inquiry concept and builds background knowledge. Next, have each inquiry circle work together to discuss major themes, concepts, and ideas that inspired them, disturbed them, or caught their attention in the immersion experience. They may make a list, collage, or graphic organizer to capture the ideas as they discuss them.
Reflection Inquiry community	Ask each circle to take a few minutes to decide on a few key interesting ideas they want to share with the inquiry community. Each inquiry circle then shares some key ideas as they refer to their list, collage, or graphic organizer to show examples. The learning team may want to provide questions to guide the reflection to help students choose the most salient information and interesting ideas. See Figure 5.1.

Figure 5.2 Immerse Model Session Plan

Notes:	Museum exhibitions are often organized by themes within a topic. For this reason, they make excellent immersion experiences. The ideas are already organized and presented to students in discrete themes that use concrete examples with images, objects, and artwork. Student can also virtually visit online exhibitions to see the same content without leaving the school, although the experience is not as compelling. Works of fiction, particularly historical fiction for humanities and science fiction for scientific study, are also good immersion experiences where themes lead to fruitful discussion. Reading a work of fiction may mean that immersion lasts for a few weeks, rather than being completed in one or two sessions.

Figure 5.2 Immerse Model Session Plan (*Continued*)

EXAMPLE SESSION PLAN

OPEN - **IMMERSE** - EXPLORE - IDENTIFY - GATHER - CREATE- SHARE - EVALUATE

Immerse - Bridge Basics

Learning Goals: Connect to content, discover interesting ideas, build background knowledge
Location: Library
Team: Math/School librarian/Science

Starter Time: 10 minutes Bridge Basic Posters available in Bridge Essentials for Educators, pp. 14–18.	In advance: Hang up posters of each basic bridge type around the library. Librarian creates a bookmarked site for the class that features bridges. The librarian also gathers other resources. Converse in the inquiry community: Think about the last time you remember crossing a bridge. Where were you? How were you travelling— on foot, by car, bicycle, bus, or train? What were your impressions? Did you notice the bridge? Ask your students to consider the definition of a bridge and what structures they consider to be bridges. Compose inquiry journal: Have students draw a sketch in their inquiry journals of what comes to mind when they think of a bridge. Ask students to think about other obstacles bridges can span and brainstorm a list (overpasses, trestle, etc.). Usually when people think of bridges, they think of structures spanning water. Ask students if they know of any bridges in their local area or famous bridges elsewhere.
Worktime Time: 30 minutes Refer students to the books and Internet sites listed in the resources section of this packet and to a bookmarking tool of the Internet sites from the unit. From p.14 of the unit.	Draw attention to each of the five basic bridge types posters.. Have students look at their journal entry. Can they identify what types of bridges they drew? Converse: Talk to your inquiry circle. Tell them which kind of bridge you think you drew: How is the one you drew like the model you see and how is it different? Look for specifics in their comparisons. http://www.nbm.org/assets/pdfs/youth-education/bridges_erpacket.pdf Next, each inquiry circle takes time to discuss and choose a type of bridge to look at in depth. Then, the inquiry circle works together to collect photos of their type of bridge from the Internet, magazines, books, or other printed materials and create posters for display in the classroom. The posters may contain additional information about the bridges, such as the distance or geographic feature they span, the materials used, date of construction, or interesting historical or anecdotal information.

Figure 5.3 Immerse Example Session Plan

Reflection Time: 15 minutes	Take a few minutes to decide on a few key things you want to share with the inquiry community. Include the key features of the bridge as students refer to the poster they made as they share examples. Questions to guide the reflection: In advance, provide this guide to students. (During poster making.) What are the key features of your type of bridge? How big were the bridges? How might someone else recognize that kind of bridge? What materials can your type of bridge be made of? What shapes make up your type of bridge? Where did you find your type of bridge? Describe the locations where your bridges were found.
Notes: Librarian creates bookmarked site for the class and gathers other resources.	Materials: poster board, glue sticks, magazines for cutting, computers bookmarked sites. This session is a way of bringing the museum to you because it uses a museum-based lesson to immerse in an understanding of bridges. It may take more time to complete. This session provides the students opportunities to think about what students know and helps them to build background knowledge together. This is the purpose of the immerse sessions. With this knowledge of bridges, students are equipped as an inquiry community to ask educated questions for inquiry after they explore their own interests and ideas in the next phase.

Figure 5.3 Immerse Example Session Plan (*Continued*)

Explore
- **Explore interesting ideas**
- **Look around**
- **Dip in**

6

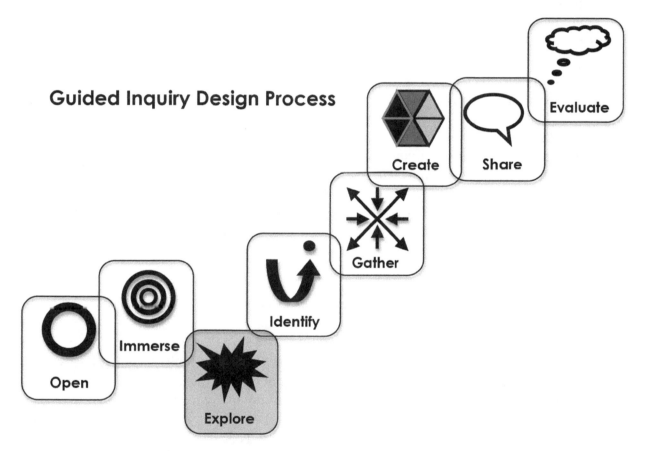

Guided Inquiry Design Process

Open — Immerse — Explore — Identify — Gather — Create — Share — Evaluate

In the Explore phase in Guided Inquiry, students browse through various sources of information to explore interesting ideas and prepare to develop their inquiry questions. In this critical early phase of constructing new learning, students need to explore ideas rather than accumulate facts. The learning team guides students to browse and scan a variety of sources. Students dip in to a few sources to make sense of the information they find and raise lots of additional questions.

In Explore, students survey a wide range of sources, read when they find something interesting, and reflect on questions that begin to shape their inquiry. Students often become overwhelmed by all the information and confused by the ideas that don't fit together. The learning team guides students to keep an open mind as they explore and reflect on new information. Guiding students through exploring leads them to form a meaningful inquiry question.

The Research

Exploration Stage of the Information Search Process

In the Exploration stage of the Information Search Process (ISP), the students' task is to explore information on the general topic with the intent of finding a focus. As students explore information about their topics, they frequently become confused by the inconsistencies and incompatibilities of information in sources with different perspectives and differing points of view. Information doesn't match their preconceived notions about their topics. Feelings of confusion and uncertainty often become threatening. Some students want to drop their topics at this point. For most students, this is the most difficult stage of the ISP.

Students often express annoyance that they aren't moving along more quickly and feel they are procrastinating. When information doesn't fit together or match what they expect, they have the sense that something is going wrong. They are confronted with the complicated task of working through the facts and ideas to form a focused perspective to pursue. But many think they are merely collecting information on their topic and hurriedly copying text without giving much thought to the ideas they are encountering.

The ISP studies found that a common problem is that students skip over the Exploration and Formulation stages and attempt to move on to the Collection stage without having formed a focus for their research. The Exploration stage of the ISP implicates an important zone of intervention for Guided Inquiry. At this stage, students are guided in exploring to identify an inquiry question with strategies and support in this early stage of learning when information and new ideas don't fit together smoothly.

Explore in Guided Inquiry

Explore is an essential phase in the inquiry process that is often misunderstood. It is at this stage that students most need guidance and when they are most likely to be left on their own. It is when critical learning takes place, and yet some students are likely to feel they are wasting time. It is a difficult stage of the inquiry process and one that is frequently overlooked entirely. This is a time when students can become confused and frustrated. They often don't know where or how to begin and expect the pieces to come together smoothly. Explore sessions need to be designed to give students realistic expectations, exploring strategies, and guidance along the way.

 Although Explore is completely different from Gather, it is often confused with the Gather phase. When gathering strategies, such as detailed note taking, are applied in Explore, students are likely to get bogged down in one source and mindlessly take copious notes without thinking about meaning. Without guidance, students can easily confuse Explore search strategies used early in the inquiry process with gathering strategies used after they have identified a clear inquiry question.

Students begin the Explore phase with some interesting ideas they have selected from the Immerse sessions. These general ideas give them a starting point for their search for information.

They are ready to explore a variety of sources of information in the library and online. The school librarian can lead the team in guiding students through this phase. It takes time for learners to construct a personal understanding from various sources of information to form a clear inquiry question to pursue. Explore is designed to give students the time to explore their ideas without pressure to make it all fit together and to raise lots of questions without pressure to choose one to center on before they are ready.

Guided Inquiry includes a number of tested strategies for guiding your students' exploration. These strategies are designed to slow the process down and move students from quickly gathering facts to the thinking and reflecting that is needed for developing a good inquiry question. They will need to look around and dip in as they search for information. This chapter describes how to use the Design Framework to apply those strategies for guiding your students' inquiry through the Explore phase. Remember, there are feelings as well as thoughts and actions to consider while guiding your students through the Explore phase of the inquiry process.

Explore Interesting Ideas

The background knowledge that students build in the Immerse phase is essential for the Explore phase of inquiry. Exploring strategies are designed to put the ideas generated in the Immerse sessions to work. For example, Immerse sessions that expose students to a museum exhibit or a dynamic historical fiction stimulate them to think about lots of interesting ideas to investigate. Explore sessions are designed to follow the immersion experience when students return to the classroom or have completed their reading or other immersion into core content. They begin by reflecting, discussing, and writing about all of the interesting ideas they discovered. The team organizes students into functional groupings around those interesting ideas in inquiry circles. Once they have some shared knowledge in the inquiry community and begin to make connections to an area of interest within the general content, students are ready to explore these interesting ideas and look for lots of questions that will lead to identifying a meaningful inquiry question.

The team designs Explore sessions so that students can investigate their ideas to see what will lead to an inquiry question. The exploratory search will help students to see which ideas are worth digging into deeper and which are dead ends. These investigations may open unexpected new ideas and lead to new discoveries. Explore is still in the beginning of the inquiry process when students need to stay open to all possibilities. Explore is a time to continue to establish third space by encouraging students to make personal connections to the content and raise questions that matter to them.

Look Around: Browsing a Variety of Sources

The main "look around" exploring strategy is browsing. Create an environment for browsing where students can browse, scan, and skim lots of sources. Google Search and Wikipedia have become a common practice in everyday information seeking. It would be useful to explain how these common resources work so students know their benefits and limitations for everyday

STOP AND JOT

When you come across a good idea or a question occurs to you, get in the habit of stopping to jot it down in your inquiry journal. You don't need to go into detail at this point. Use this form or make two columns in your journal with the page number in the margin and jotted notes beside it.

This is important for keeping track of where you found the idea so that you can find it again when you want to. In addition, you will record the citation in your inquiry log so that later, when you are further along in your inquiry, you can cite the source that you used.

Source:	
Page Number	Ideas and questions

Source:	
Page Number	Ideas and questions

Figure 6.1 Stop and Jot

From *Guided Inquiry Design: A Framework for Inquiry in Your School* by Carol C. Kuhlthau, Leslie K. Maniotes, and Ann K. Caspari. Santa Barbara, CA: Libraries Unlimited. Copyright © 2012.

and academic inquiry. Typically, the school librarian will take the lead on designing exploring search strategies and developing sources for looking around to explore interesting ideas for questions about the topic. There is a range of quality sources for browsing. An exploratory search can be designed as a trail through quality sources that provides an overview of what is generally available on the topic. The school librarian, in consultation with the other members of the learning team, can prepare a digital library for the inquiry unit that includes high-quality databases; web sites; and digitized materials from libraries, museums, and archives that pertain specifically to the content of the unit to supplement the materials available in school. The team will need to thoughtfully design exploratory search strategies and guide students in browsing because too many sources all at once can overwhelm students at this stage.

Students need to be guided to understand that information doesn't fit together smoothly during exploring. Sources often are inconsistent and incompatible and not exactly what students expect to find. Taking detailed notes at this time is counterproductive to the thinking process. Students learn and use reading strategies for browsing. Browsing strategies, like skim and scan, give students a sense of what's there, how much is there, what's the point of view, what's new to them, and what might be worth knowing more about. Explore concentrates on who, what, where, and when questions that lead to developing deeper why and how inquiry questions. Students begin keeping an inquiry log listing sources that might be useful to check later in the Gather phase.

During the Explore phase, the learning team introduces a stop and jot approach to taking notes in inquiry journals (Figure 6.1). This approach is a good way to think about this kind of journaling, which captures ideas as they are encountered in an information search. A good inquiry question develops from the ideas students come across in browsing. Stop and jot is a good way to capture these ideas.

Dip In: Relax, Read, and Reflect

The main dip-in exploring strategies are relax, read, and reflect. Relaxing may seem like an unusual attitude to recommend to students in school. However, when students rush through exploring, their thoughts about their ideas have little opportunity to evolve or develop. As learners slow down and relax, they can read and reflect on the information they are exploring. They can begin to define and extend their ideas and raise questions. While assuming a relaxed attitude, they are centering their attention on exploring for a meaningful question. Again, they are not taking detailed notes at this time.

In Explore, the learning team guides an inquiry stance for the inquiry community. The inquiry stance in Explore is a calm, reflective tone, not rushed or deadline oriented. The team creates an environment that values a thoughtful, attentive, interested approach, rather than a mindless, indiscriminate, accumulation of sources. The team asks students, What is interesting as you dip in and read? What are you finding that you'd like to tell someone else about? What questions come to mind? Have students jot these down in their inquiry journal.

Reading to become informed and raise questions is a primary strategy for exploring. Through reading and engaging with other types of texts, students define their ideas and extend their understanding. Their reading leads them to note interesting facts, ideas, and questions that they jot down in their inquiry journal. Sometimes they discover opposing points of view.

Without careful reading in Explore, rarely can a good inquiry question be formulated in the Identify phase of the inquiry process. Dipping in to reading and reflecting in an inquiry journal helps students to develop a meaningful inquiry question (Figure 6.2). Before writing, it is often helpful to talk with a partner about our own thinking. This pairing is an efficacious way to help students compose in their journals about the areas that matter to them in the Explore phase.

The journal entry for Explore uses recall and reflect. Students recall something that struck them as they were reading, reflect on their thoughts, ideas, and feelings and compose their thoughts in their journal. They then turn to their inquiry circles to converse about the ideas and questions that most interested, intrigued, or disturbed them.

As students reflect on their reading, their thoughts evolve. Thoughts are extended through reflections in the inquiry journal and in conversations in inquiry circles as students reflect on what they have read and share their ideas and questions with others in the inquiry community. Many students describe having an "aha" experience of ideas coming together when they least expect it. The Design Framework always includes a reflective Explore phase where students have an opportunity to have that "aha" moment. The inquiry tools provide multiple opportunities for students to have these "aha" experiences as they converse and compose to capture them. Students need considerable guidance in exploring to gain strategies for germinating ideas and questions in this formative time in the inquiry process. Through exploring, they become aware of their own learning process, which is an important aspect of learning how to learn.

The team will set up an environment for exploring that allows for different styles of relaxing and different styles of learning. Some students may want to sit on the floor, while others may prefer to sit in a cozy nook. Some students cannot get into a relaxed frame of mind unless they are allowed to move about the room or walk. Others will need quiet places. The learning team will plan where the exploration sessions will occur to accommodate the learners. The school library as the learning commons may best provide for all of these different modes. The important concept here is that ideas about the topic need some time to germinate enough for students to form a good inquiry question.

 It may seem to some students that little is happening and that they are wasting time. Some students have little patience for the reflective thought process of the Exploration stage. Some feel they are "procrastinating" at this point and want to "get on with it." But as a more experienced student in the ISP studies explained, "The mind doesn't take everything and put it into order automatically and that's it. Understanding that is the biggest help" (Kuhlthau 2004). It is difficult for even experienced researchers to know when they are germinating an idea and when they are avoiding work on a difficult project.

Reading, journaling, and reflecting are companion activities that enable ideas to grow into meaningful inquiry questions. The team makes explicit the importance of reflection. As students become aware of their need to reflect, they will learn to allow time for this. They will also become aware of the necessity to read during the inquiry process to promote their thinking rather than saving all of the reading for the end. The learning team is always working to have students move toward becoming more self-directed learners.

The school librarian organizes an exploratory search for students to browse a number of different sources. The example of an Explore session provided introduces sources for browsing content using a stations approach. After engaging in an immersion experience, students

PAIR SHARE PROTOCOL

Pair Share Protocol Prompts	Getting ready to identify inquiry question
As you dip in and read, write down what seems interesting to you.	This is interesting . . .
Write why you think it is interesting.	This is interesting because . . .
Read over what you have written and write the things you would like to tell someone else about.	I would like to tell about . . .
Pair Share **Partner A:** Shares. **Partner B:** Listens and takes notes. **Partner B:** Shares. **Partner A:** Listens and takes notes.	Share with your partner and take notes. Telling helps to clarify your ideas for forming a good inquiry question.
Partners exchange notes.	Your partner's notes on what you shared can give you insight for forming possible inquiry questions.
Reflect on what you found interesting and how you described it to your partner and think about possible questions to look into further.	Write three possible questions that you would like to explore further.

Figure 6.2 Explore Pair Share Protocol

From *Guided Inquiry Design: A Framework for Inquiry in Your School* by Carol C. Kuhlthau, Leslie K. Maniotes, and Ann K. Caspari. Santa Barbara, CA: Libraries Unlimited. Copyright © 2012.

brainstorm ideas that they are interested in and create a list for exploring. Each station introduces a different source with instructions on how to use the source and how to cite it in the student inquiry log. The example session plan has eight stations including current magazines/print and web-based materials, databases, Google Earth/maps/atlases, selected web sites, web-based images, print and on-line encyclopedia articles, podcasts, and materials in the science section of the library. As students progress through the stations browsing sources to explore their interesting ideas, they are looking for a few sources to dip into.

The learning team may organize the stations around themes to guide students through the exploring session. For example, in an inquiry unit on problems of migratory birds, some themes that may emerge are geography of where the birds fly, how far they go, changing habitats, and endangered species. Stations may be organized both by content themes and by types of sources. Students need to browse with the intent of finding something to dip into to identify their inquiry question.

What is the Team Doing?

The learning team uses modeling, listening, and encouraging to foster third space in inquiry learning. In the Explore phase, the team models a variety of searching and reading strategies. They listen for students' ideas and feelings and encourage students to take time to explore.

Modeling

The team models an inquiry stance; exploratory search strategies that incorporate browsing, scanning, skimming a variety of sources; dipping into read and reflect; jotting ideas and reflecting in inquiry journals; and choosing sources to record in inquiry logs.

Listening

The team listens for developing ideas that lead to potential questions for further investigation. They listen to students to determine feelings of being overwhelmed or frustrated by all the information and set students at ease by explaining that uncertainty is normal for this phase. As indicated by the ISP research, these feelings are typical, and the team can reassure students when they know they are feeling this way.

Encouraging

The team encourages a relaxed atmosphere for exploration and allows time for exploring to take place. Students need encouragement to keep going in the Explore phase of Guided Inquiry when they become confused by information and ideas that don't fit together. The team encourages students to read, relax, and reflect and to explore what is interesting. Using these prompts, What is interesting as you dip in and read? What are you finding that you'd like to tell someone else about? What questions come to mind?, the team guides students to explore interesting ideas with the purpose of generating inquiry questions worthy of pursuit. The team guides students to reflect on their explorations by responding in their inquiry journals.

Assessing

The team assesses students' progress in exploring ideas by evidence in their inquiry journals, conversations in inquiry circles, and interactions in the inquiry community to offer specific guidance for exploring to develop inquiry questions. The school librarian assesses inquiry logs to guide use of quality sources for browsing and inquiry journals to advise on sources for dipping in.

What is the Learner Doing?

During Explore, the students use tools to choose, compose, collaborate, and converse. The inquiry log is used to track and document information sources. The journal is used to jot down ideas and compose in order to explore and prepare for inquiry circles. Students gather in inquiry circles to converse and collaborate and continue the inquiry as they share in the inquiry community.

Inquiry Logs for Tracking Sources: Choosing

The inquiry log is a simple but useful tool (Figure 6.3). You will see the benefit for students as they track their journey and the choices they make. It is also beneficial for the learning team to monitor at a glance how students are making choices about their information use.

Inquiry logs are introduced in Explore as a tool for keeping track of the students' choices of sources in the inquiry process. The students log sources that they think are useful or may be useful. As they find sources in those two categories, students record the date, citation of source, and thoughts they have as they browse and dip in. In the thoughts column of the journal, students write a personal note, a brief comment, or a question about what is interesting. Thoughts should be a short, quick entry that is easy to refer to later.

Students' choices are evidenced by an entry in the log as well as a check in the "maybe" column of the journal for sources they are thinking about. Most choices fall in the "maybe" column in Explore because students aren't yet sure of the direction of the inquiry. Inquiry logs are an important tool for tracking a search and for reflecting on the sequence and usefulness of sources. Choosing isn't a simple task and requires some guidance. The school librarian guides students in making good choices within the vast number of resources available. Inquiry logs are productive tools for tracking the choices in the inquiry journey which develops information literacy over time.

The log can be kept with the journal so that all information remains in one place and is easy to access. This is increasingly important as students progress through the inquiry process. The log will be brought out again in the Gather phase. For younger students, the log can be stapled into the journal for safe-keeping. The log can also be in digital format.

Inquiry Journals for Explore

In the Explore phase, the inquiry journal is used for jotting down ideas from sources of information. Inquiry journals become a list of questions, facts, and ideas that occur to students as they work through the Explore phase. The inquiry journal is a tool for formulating thoughts that lead to developing a meaningful inquiry question. The journal continues to be used to prepare for conversation in the inquiry circles that help students make decisions about questions for

INQUIRY LOG

Use this inquiry log from the Explore stage through the Create stage.

	Explore	**Gather**
Track your choices through the inquiry.	As you explore, check the box if you might use the source for your inquiry. ✔ "Maybe"	As you gather, check the box if you will use the source for your inquiry. ✔ "Use it"
Track the reading strategies you use.	As you explore, place an x after the sources you dipped in to.	As you gather, mark an * after the core sources you read deeply.

Cite all your sources.

	Source Citation	Maybe ✔ / Dip in x	Notes: What makes it useful?	Use it ✔ / Go deep *
1				
2				
3				
4				
5				
6				
7				
8				
9				
10				

Figure 6.3 Inquiry Log

further investigation. Inquiry journals are used for reflecting after dip-in reading. Students are guided to use the journal for a "recall, summarize, paraphrase, and extend exercise," that is, an exercise that leads to developing an inquiry question.

A good framework for reflecting on the inquiry in the journal is to recall, summarize, paraphrase, and extend, as follows:

- **Recall:** Think about what you remember about immersing.
- **Summarize:** Tell important, interesting ideas from what you remember but not every detail.
- **Paraphrase:** Write ideas down in your own words.
- **Extend:** Identify the important, interesting ideas that you want to know more about.

By using this simple framework, students stop and think about what they have read. Sometimes they know more than they realize, and getting them to write down what they got out of a reading provides that small but necessary time to reflect and take it all in.

Inquiry Circles for Exploring

Learners continue to work in inquiry circles to collaborate and communicate their understandings with a small group. Regular meeting times gives students the routine that supports their exploration, reflection, and activity in the inquiry community. Being required to share with others makes students hold each other accountable for the work and helps to keep everyone on track. Inquiry circles work in tandem with inquiry journals. Students bring their completed journal entries to the inquiry circle, providing a basis for the conversation based in generating thoughts, growing ideas, and choosing interests in a small group. Conversations in inquiry circles are shared with the entire inquiry community as students learn more and begin to form inquiry questions that the whole community finds worthwhile.

Inquiry Community for Exploring

While exploring, the inquiry community continues to strengthen and grow. The learners continue to experience ways in which sharing ideas and information back and forth can enrich their understanding and help to develop ideas that lead to formulating inquiry questions. The inquiry community continues to work together, even as each learner begins to develop individual understanding and questions. In the earlier example about migrating birds, the learners worked together in the community to develop important, engaging, or troubling inquiry questions about migrating birds. Large group reflection with many voices and conversations in smaller, more intimate groups are ways that learners can puzzle out what they are most interested in investigating further.

Ideas for Explore Sessions

Explore usually is arranged in the library where resources are located, computers are available for online access, and space is provided for a variety of exploratory search sessions. These sessions provide opportunities for students to browse and dip in to explore a range of sources. Some ideas for designing sessions that guide students to explore are described throughout this chapter.

Learning stations can be used to explore a variety of themes within a subject using different sources. Stations are framed around the learning needs of students. The stations can provide an introduction to a range of different types of sources or demonstrate many different ways to use one type of source. When designing exploring sessions, the entire learning team needs to consider when is the best time to introduce sources for students to use in the inquiry unit. If students have not had prior experience with a type of source, it is useful to introduce them within the meaningful context of an inquiry unit. For example, atlases are useful when the inquiry is about a place. When students have to use a source such as an atlas to locate something important for their inquiry, learning is more likely to endure than when introduced in an "atlas lesson" that is out of context. Stations can be efficiently designed to overlap sources, skills, and strategies. For example, stations give students time and space to explore different sources while, at the same time, introducing them to citation format for entries into the inquiry log.

Explore sessions can be designed to let students look around with opportunities to browse and scan a variety of sources (Figures 6.4 and 6.5). These browsing sessions must be strategically placed within the inquiry and include some type of tracking device, such as exit cards or the inquiry log, so that the team can keep track of the variety of sources and information students have tapped into during the session. Some students may need open, informal browsing strategies, while others may need more structure. The flexibility of open browsing and a more structured approach requires knowing the learners, where they are within the process, and their individual learning needs.

It is important to create access to a wide range of appropriate interesting materials that students can browse, scan, and skim. A collection of materials may be prearranged for students using web 2.0 tools such as jogtheweb.com or livebinder.com, as well as other social bookmarking tools, to direct students to sources that illuminate a specific idea, concept, or theme. A successful exploratory search is dependent on access to a wide variety of quality information sources. Designing access to high-quality texts in many formats is essential for Guided Inquiry.

Once students find something interesting, time and space must be designed into the Explore sessions so that they can use the dip-in strategy and relax, read, and reflect. Create a comfortable space to heighten concentration for reading and reflecting. A regular routine of journaling during Explore is recommended as a reflection, thought tool. Explore sessions are designed to provide open, receptive environment for thinking and talking about ideas and emerging questions in the inquiry circles and within the whole inquiry community.

What's Next? Identifying

The learning team guides students in exploring information to construct meaningful focused questions. Immersing and exploring that leads to identifying an inquiry question doesn't always need to be drawn out. It actually might take a short time. However, the Explore phase can't be skipped. At the close of Explore, students have a clearer idea of how to focus their inquiry questions. They are prepared to identify a direction for their inquiry by forming an inquiry question in the next stage of the process.

MODEL SESSION PLAN

OPEN - IMMERSE - **EXPLORE** - IDENTIFY - GATHER - CREATE- SHARE - EVALUATE

Learning Goals: Explore interesting ideas, look around, and browse a variety of
    sources; dip in
Location: School library
Team: Learning team

This Explore session uses stations to help students look around and browse a variety of
sources to select from for something to dip in, read, and reflect on in order to identify
a meaningful inquiry question. Alternately, the team might decide to use one type
of source in stations to familiarize students with how to find information in that type of
source.

Starter Time: 5 minutes	Before this session each student has some interesting ideas to explore. Start with three examples of the variety of sources you are providing students in the stations. Share the three examples and discuss with students how they differ and how they think using a variety of sources can enhance their work. Explain that you have set up stations to help students explore their interesting ideas by browsing a variety of sources. Have students quickly "turn and talk" about their immerse ideas. Demonstrate that each station has a different source for them to look over in order to explore the interesting ideas they listed in the Immerse phase of the inquiry process. Explain that each station has a color card to show how to cite the source in their inquiry log.
Worktime Time: 30 minutes Note: After this session is introduced in the starter, the worktime and reflection may be repeated to allow	Stations are organized around a carefully selected variety of sources for looking around and browsing. Of course, sources are carefully selected for this task and will depend on the content of the unit of study, students' learning needs, and the resources in your school. The students' task is to look around at the sources in each station to get an idea of what is there. At each station, they will make a decision about whether or not this source follows their interest. They will cite sources in their inquiry log, mark their usefulness, and then find something they want to dip into in that source. Dipping in is a strategy that will help students explore more deeply and will prepare them to identify possible inquiry questions.

Figure 6.4 Explore Model Session Plan

adequate time for browsing stations to select a source for dipping into. Inquiry Log	Stations may be loaded onto laptops. Stations may include: • Books that highlight sections of the library • Current materials, magazines, online newspapers, news clips, or videos • Databases • Encyclopedia articles, both print and web-based, for example, world book, Wikipedia • Maps and atlases, both print and web-based, for example, Google Earth • Web sites • Videos, podcasts, T.E.D. talks, virtual tours • Images, art, photos, posters, both print and web-based, for example, those from the Smithsonian • American Memory Library of Congress: letters, diaries, music scores, documents • Music recordings Questions to have students keep in mind while they are browsing sources include • "What do you want to know more about?" and • "Which sources do you want to spend a little more time with?" As students browse, they are looking to explore their interesting ideas. By the end of the session, each student will have selected at least one source to dip into and determine what to reflect on. In addition, each source will be documented in their inquiry log.
Reflection Time: 10 minutes	Inquiry circles: Discussion Have students gather in inquiry circles for a conversation to share their ideas and get a response from the group. Each member shares: • What sources would I like to dip into further? • Why do I think it might be a useful source? • How does it provide variety and multiple perspectives to the work? Members of the circle will follow with questions of clarification on rationale or content and probe to see if they have other wonderings that might help the speaker. During session closure, students will bring back to the inquiry community ideas they discovered or discussed in small groups about a variety of sources and how looking around helped them. (Debriefing how "looking around" helped them takes students to a meta-cognitive level. This helps students to process the inquiry learning and makes them aware of the strategy you are providing them that will help them learn how to learn in future tasks.)

Figure 6.4 Explore Model Session Plan (*Continued*)

Notes:	The look-around sessions are followed by dip-in sessions with relaxed time for reading and reflecting. During dip-in sessions, students will dig deeper and begin to jot reactions and questions in their inquiry journals (see Figure 6.1 Stop and jot). Explore is a time to browse and dip in to find emerging inquiry questions. Students are not yet ready to take detailed notes. Remember this is a time when students easily get overwhelmed and confused. You will need to be aware of their confusion and be there to help.

Figure 6.4 Explore Model Session Plan (*Continued*)

EXAMPLE SESSION PLAN

OPEN - IMMERSE - **EXPLORE** - IDENTIFY - GATHER - CREATE- SHARE - EVALUATE

Learning Goals: Explore interesting ideas, look around, and browse a variety of sources
Location: School library
Team: Science teacher, school librarian, social studies teacher
Inquiry Unit: Bird migration

This Explore session uses stations organized around students' interests to help them look around and browse a variety of sources. The sources are organized so that students can select something to dip into, read, reflect on, and identify a meaningful inquiry question.

Starter Time: 5 minutes	Begin the session by explaining the stations in a two-minute tour. Here's a sample introduction: "We have seven stations that will help you think and learn more about some of the ideas you had about migratory birds. Go to two stations with the task of finding out what is interesting. Jot down your ideas and questions in your inquiry journals." Model how to cite the source in the inquiry logs. (Document camera) "Each station has a color card that provides a sample of how to cite that source. Write down the source you explore in your inquiry log."
Worktime Time: 30 minutes Two stations/ 15 minutes each Inquiry journal Inquiry log	While students are exploring the stations, guide them to use their inquiry journal to record what they hear, read, see, or discover that is interesting. Encourage them to add their reactions and any questions they have about bird migration. Note which students need help citing sources in the inquiry log. Stations: Nests: web-based image search http://nationalzoo.si.edu/scbi/migratorybirds/science_article/default.cfm?id=19 Migration: Current issue http://nationalzoo.si.edu/SCBI/MigratoryBirds/Research/Marra/development-changes-bird-songs.cfm The story of the NJ Willet http://nationalzoo.si.edu/scbi/migratory birds/research/willet/ http://nationalzoo.si.edu/scbi/migratorybirds/podcast/ (podcast of the Willet article) http://news.nationalgeographic.com/news/2009/02/090216-bird-migration-missions.html Identification: books 500–590s Maps: North America/South America How far do birds travel? Track where and how far they went.

Figure 6.5 Explore Example Session Plan

	<u>Habitat:</u> http://nationalzoo.si.edu/scbi/migratorybirds/research/urban_ecology/ http://nationalzoo.si.edu/scbi/migratorybirds/research/neighborhood_nestwatch/data_summary.cfm <u>Bird calls; sounds change:</u> http://nationalzoo.si.edu/SCBI/Migratory Birds/Research/Marra/development-changes-bird-songs.cfm <u>Birdwatching; spotting migratory birds:</u> http://www.allaboutbirds.org/page.aspx?pid=1200 http://birds.audubon.org/ Open stations for individual exploration.
Reflection Time: 10 minutes Inquiry circles	Have students get into inquiry circles and share the most interesting idea. Reflect together on questions and problems to learn more about. "Jot down the questions that come up in your conversation in your journal." Designate a scribe who will jot down the questions that come up in the inquiry circle conversation to share with the inquiry community. (These lists of questions can be assigned like an "exit card" for the team to monitor direction and progress of the inquiry.)
Notes:	Students return to the school library to continue exploration. The goal is not to have them rotate through each station but to thoroughly explore their own interests to identify a meaningful question or a problem to pursue.

Figure 6.5 Explore Example Session Plan (*Continued*)

Identify

- **Pause and ponder**
- **Identify inquiry question**
- **Decide direction**

7

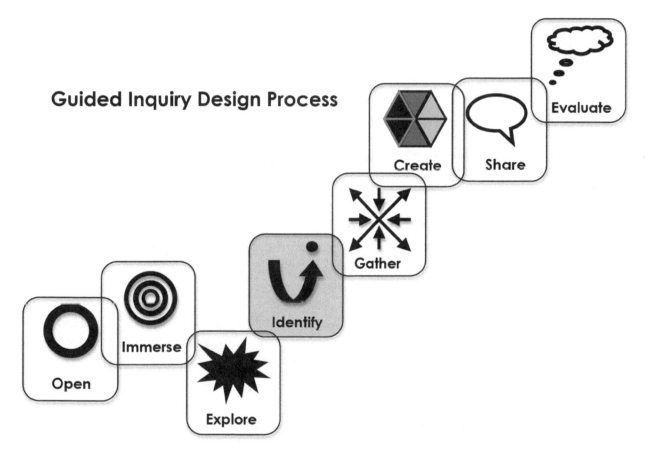

Guided Inquiry Design Process

Open · Immerse · Explore · Identify · Gather · Create · Share · Evaluate

In Identify, learners pause in the inquiry process to ask a meaningful inquiry question. In Guided Inquiry, they have had lots of preparation for this phase. Students are ready to identify an important question for their inquiry because of the time they have spent immersing and exploring to build enough background knowledge to ask many meaningful questions.

The main task during the Identify phase is to construct an inquiry question from the interesting ideas, pressing problems, and emerging themes students have explored in various sources of information. The team introduces strategies that enable each student to sort through information and ideas to clearly articulate a meaningful inquiry question that will frame the rest of the inquiry.

The Research

Formulation Stage of the Information Search Process

The students' task in the Formulation stage of the Information Search Process (ISP) is to form a focus from the information found in the Exploration stage. Formulation of a focus marks the turning point of the ISP when feelings of uncertainty and confusion diminish and confidence increases. The types of information students are seeking also changes. Before students form a focus, they explore general information on the topic. After they identify a focus, they gather specific information about their focus. They emerge from a sense of confusion and feelings of doubt that they are on the right track to a sense of purpose and feelings of confidence in their ability to complete their task.

Students who build background knowledge and identify ideas in the Exploration stage are prepared to form a focused perspective of the general topic. Students who do not form a focus continue to collect general information and often experience difficulty when they begin to write and prepare to present their findings. By forming a focus, students identify an area of concentration in which their ideas continue to grow and evolve from the information they encounter in the Collection stage. The focus does not remain static but continues to take shape throughout the Collection stage. In forming a focus, students find it helpful to read over notes for themes and ideas and to reflect, discuss, and write about these ideas. Four criteria used to form a focus are:

- Personal interest: What is personally interesting?
- Assignment requirements: What is the requirement of the assignment?
- Information available: How much information is available?
- Time: How much time do I have?

The Formulation stage of the ISP indicates a zone of intervention in Guided Inquiry to enable students to identify an important question from the interesting ideas they have explored to give direction for gathering information for deep personal learning.

Identify in Guided Inquiry

We have reached the time in Guided Inquiry for learners to identify a meaningful inquiry question. The groundwork for asking the question has been laid. The ISP shows that it takes time to learn enough about a subject area to be able to ask a meaningful inquiry question. In Guided Inquiry, students are very engaged in the phases that lead up to identifying an important question. They gain solid background knowledge. They explore a wide range of interesting ideas. Now they are prepared to ask a well-formed inquiry question.

At the Identify phase, the emphasis is on forming meaningful inquiry question. Identifying an important focused question is essential for personal learning and deep understanding to take place in the inquiry process. For students, a meaningful question is, what do I care about and want to learn about? All students may not be ready to identify an inquiry question at the same time. The learning team will need to be aware of when students are ready for this decision. Some may need more time exploring. The team will need to give individual guidance to these students and help them move along in the inquiry process. The inquiry circles can provide a support to students who need more time to work on their ideas before forming an inquiry question.

Pause and Ponder

This is a critical turning point in Guided Inquiry when students identify their inquiry question, just as forming a focus is in the ISP. It is the time to pause for reflection on all that has been learned so far and to identify an important question to concentrate on before moving on. Explore will have broadened students understanding of interesting ideas and raised lots of possible questions to pursue. This turning point is a time to review, reflect, and identify where to take the inquiry next.

Care needs to be taken not to press students to Identify a focused question too early in the inquiry process before they are ready. Too often, Identify is skipped altogether and students continue with a broad general question all the way through the process without forming a personal perspective to pursue at any point. Without Identify, students fail to make the inquiry their own and to gain deep understanding.

Identify Meaningful Questions

After Explore, students know enough to ask and wonder in a more informed way, rather than taking a stab in the dark and seizing on something that really doesn't matter. Through the Explore phase, the learning team has an essential role in guiding students by being continually on the look out for productive inquiry questions that arise in journals, circles, and the inquiry community. Inquiry questions cannot be answered simply. Inquiry questions open up interesting possibilities for investigation and research. They raise curiosity and inspire students to want to learn and connect with what students already know and care about. Inquiry questions prompt students to wonder and speculate and are formed from the information and ideas uncovered while exploring.

Inquiry implies that students will address a question, not necessarily seek an answer. A meaningful question for inquiry will have an easy answer. Formulating a focused question is a complex task. Important questions lead beyond fact-finding to gathering factual information to support, extend, or define ideas that deepen understanding. Throughout Explore, students built factual knowledge using the lower-order questions of who, what, where, and when. Now they have some factual knowledge and can ask higher-order questions of why and how. What, when, who questions lead to why and how questions, such as, why does this happen? how does this work? Why and how questions lead to interpreting facts and coming up with a creative understanding to share. Although this is a good rule of thumb, it is a simplistic view of the possibilities. "What if" questions are open ended and require students to speculate beyond the facts and information given. The main point is that the questions go beyond gathering facts about something to asking how and why something is important. The learning team plays a major role in guiding students to compose questions that matter.

How do shadows work? How does the shape of a shadow change when the object is rotated and moved closer or farther from a light source? Why does the moon seem to change shape in the sky and how do shadows relate to the change in how the moon looks? Even very young students who have immersed in how shadows work by watching a video of *Sid the Science Kid* and then using simple objects and flashlights may be ready to apply this information to understanding the relationships between a more complex group of objects like the sun, earth, and moon. In the immersion sessions, students may notice that objects get bigger when moved closer to a light source and the shadow of an object can change shape when rotated depending on where the light source falls on the object. Without that initial immersion experience, students would not have the background knowledge to formulate questions or understand the complexity of the phases of the moon. The learning team helps the students to find the words for the questions in which they are interested. They pay attention during the immersion experiences for signs of developing inquiry questions that can be brought out in the reflection portion at the end of the session.

In the Explore chapter, students explored inquiry questions related to bird migrations. After building background knowledge that birds migrate, some biology of birds, and information about the geography of bird migration, students are ready to identify questions about bird migration that are personally interesting. Do migratory birds travel close to where I live or to places I have been or know about? How far away do specific birds travel? What are the effects of urban development on birds? How do the things people build, such as wind turbines, affect bird migration? Are all human changes to the environment harmful to birds? What are some new ways that scientists track and understand bird migration? What can people in our area do to help migratory birds or the scientists studying them?

The above example shows the wide range of questions that could arise out of the previous examples of inquiries that are found in this book. Developing questions is an important component of the first phases of the inquiry process. In Identify, students must choose the question that they will pursue for the rest of the inquiry. The next section provides criteria for making the important decision of identifying a meaningful inquiry question.

Decide on an Inquiry Question

Students may be guided to consider the following four criteria to identify an important question:

- What is interesting to me?
- What are my learning goals?
- How much information is available?
- How much time do I have?

The inquiry journal is a good place to reflect on these criteria in ISP for selecting an inquiry question.

What is Interesting to Me?

At this phase in the inquiry process, personal interest is of the utmost importance for identifying the inquiry question. Learners need to be guided to identify an inquiry question that not only seems interesting but also is important and matters to them. Personal interest is a critical factor in sustaining students' persistence in continuing through the challenges of the inquiry process to deep learning.

What are My Learning Goals?

When inquiry is designed thoughtfully, students go through the first three phases without concern for the assignment. Once students have identified a question, the assignment is introduced and learning goals can be made even more transparent with students. It is good for students to think about what they are trying to accomplish in the inquiry and what will be the outcome of their inquiry. It is important to have a goal in mind for the inquiry and to return to that goal at various points in the process. The learning goal is different from the end product. Students will be better prepared to decide on the inquiry product after they have gathered information on their question and begin to picture what they want to create to communicate their learning. At this point, they need to be guided to think about their learning goal and challenged to raise their goal beyond fact-finding to interpreting for meaning and significance. Whether the goal is fact-finding or interpreting will make a difference in the approach and decisions at every phase in the process and will impact the outcome of the inquiry. Fact-finding will result in repackaging and reporting facts. Interpreting will result in connecting facts and explaining what they mean. Interpreting will lead to deep, long-lasting understanding.

How Much Information is Available?

At this point in the inquiry process, the type of information changes from general information on the subject to specific information on the inquiry question. In Guided Inquiry, students learn to conduct different types of searches at different phases in the inquiry process to determine the availability of information. Up to this point, they have done some browsing to get an overview of what is available on the general topic and to get information on interesting ideas. After they have identified an inquiry question, their search will be limited and framed by what is available to address their question.

How Much Time Do I Have?

Time is an important factor to consider at every point in the inquiry process. When time is the main factor driving the process, it tends to limit the choices students make. Interesting ideas and meaningful questions need to be the primary force driving the inquiry process. The learning team helps students gain a sense of timing as they learn to pace their way through the phases of the inquiry process. The point is that students aren't left on their own to figure this out. Guided Inquiry is designed and paced so that students learn how to balance the pursuit of what is interesting and important to them to reach their learning goals with the information available and within the time allotted. It is designed to provide flexibility for different learning styles and the different learning needs of students.

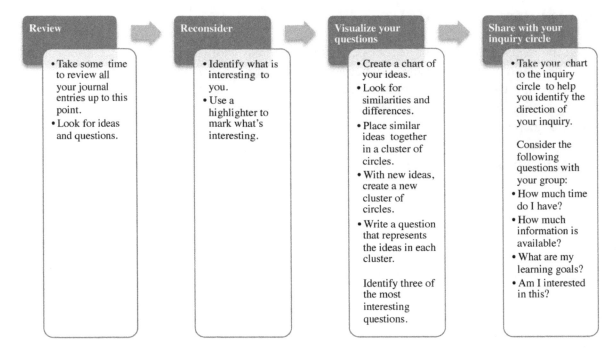

Figure 7.1 Chart to Decide Protocol

Inquiry Charts for Identifying an Inquiry Question

The learning team guides students in reviewing interesting ideas they have noted in their inquiry journals during Explore and to compose questions from these ideas. The school librarian guides students in reviewing their inquiry logs to track how much information is available and what sources seem to have the most important information. At this point in the process, inquiry circle conversations center on identifying important questions from ideas generated in Immerse and Explore.

Charting at this time is especially helpful to organize ideas and identify inquiry questions. Inquiry charts are introduced to help students link ideas and see emerging questions (Figure 7.1). Charting provides a structure for students to sort through the notes, ideas, and questions in their inquiry journals to make a decision for identifying an inquiry question. Inquiry charts present a large amount of information and ideas in a compact way that enables thinking. Inquiry charts help students visualize ideas, issues, conflicts, relationships, and strategies that emerge during exploration to identify an inquiry question. Students of all ages can benefit from visualizing their thoughts through inquiry charts. Concept maps and graphic organizers are useful with elementary and older students. Very young children can express ideas in drawings as a form of charting. With guidance, students can get into the habit of using inquiry charts to help them identify meaningful inquiry questions. (See also Figure 7.3.)

What is the Team Doing?

The learning team uses modeling, listening, and encouraging to foster third space in inquiry learning. In the Identify phase, the team models a variety of charting strategies. They listen for students' ideas and emerging questions and encourage students to take time to review and reflect.

Modeling

The team models how to create an inquiry chart that helps students sift through their ideas and identify questions worthy of further investigation. The team models the thinking process behind the inquiry chart and decision-making for identifying a meaningful inquiry question.

Listening

The team is listening for emerging inquiry questions in inquiry circles and from individuals identifying questions for inquiry, noting students who need additional help forming an important inquiry question.

Encouraging

The team encourages reflection and review of inquiry journals as a purposeful activity to come to a meaningful question. They encourage students first to consider what is most interesting, then to find similarities between ideas and to group similar ideas together. They encourage a wide variety of questioning and finally to identify one important question that will deepen student learning and sustain their interest throughout the inquiry process.

Assessing

The team is looking for evidence that the inquiry is going to move into deep learning. They are noting who needs help with this early synthesizing task to identify an inquiry question and are providing guidance and support to students who are having particular difficulty. They are checking that the interest level is high so that students have the persistence that sustains and deepens learning throughout the entire inquiry process.

What is the Learner Doing?

During Identify, the students use inquiry tools to choose a direction for the inquiry. By reviewing and reflecting on the inquiry log and the contents of the journal, students chart the ideas and information to decide on a question to pursue. Students gather in inquiry circles to converse and collaborate on their decision-making. Students continue the inquiry as they share in the inquiry community.

Inquiry Log for Reviewing Choices

Students review the choices they have made of the sources that may be useful in their inquiry. They particularly note the thoughts that they have jotted down about the sources that they found. The range of sources they have located and their initial thoughts about these sources help them to know what information is available about inquiry questions they are considering.

Inquiry Journal for Identifying an Inquiry Question

Students review their inquiry journals for the background knowledge and ideas they have accumulated in Immerse and Explore and use that information to develop their first inquiry chart. In particular, they consider the information, facts, and ideas they have written about from the sources they chose for dipping in to read and reflect. The ideas from their inquiry journals form the basis of identifying a meaningful inquiry question.

Inquiry Charts for Identifying Inquiry Question

Students develop an inquiry chart to sort through their ideas to identify possible inquiry questions. Their inquiry journals are a good source to draw from to identify questions that inform their research. They are introduced to a number of different kinds of charts and graphic organizers described in this chapter. Students take their inquiry journals to their inquiry circles for conversations prior to creating a chart to help them prioritize and think about the possibilities and promise each question holds.

Inquiry Circle: Identifying Meaningful Inquiry Questions in Small Groups

Students bring their inquiry journals to their inquiry circles to work together to help one another identify an interesting inquiry question. They use the criteria set by the inquiry community that meets the learning goals of their inquiry unit. In this way, each student is prepared to identify a meaningful question to provide a direction for the inquiry going forward.

Ideas for Identify Sessions

Graphic organizers that help students prioritize are useful tools for sorting through a lot of complex ideas. Many thinking maps and graphic organizers are available, some as web 2.0 versions that are useful for saving and sharing with others.

As students become more familiar with charting, more sophisticated forms of charts and mapping may be used. The type of charting will depend on students' level of understanding of the topic. The concept map is a handy, effective tool for students to get into the habit of using on their own for visualizing, synthesizing, and organizing multiple ideas to make a decision. Flowcharts are helpful for making "if–then" decisions. Charts enable students to picture the many ideas and questions they have explored in a concise space that fosters identifying a good inquiry question. Identify sessions in Figures 7.2 through 7.6 are designed around charting that is combined with time for reviewing journals and logs, rereading core sources, and discussing possible questions with criteria for making choices and provide opportunities for identifying meaningful inquiry questions.

What's Next? Gather

At the close of Identify, students have identified a clearly articulated question for their inquiry as they move on to the Gather phase. Their inquiry question provides direction for gathering information and learning in the next phases of the inquiry process.

MODEL SESSION PLAN

OPEN - IMMERSE - EXPLORE - **IDENTIFY** - GATHER - CREATE- SHARE - EVALUATE

Learning Goals: Pause and ponder, identify inquiry question, decide direction
Location: School library or classroom
Team: Learning team

This Identify session uses a cluster chart to identify questions that are best suited for meaningful inquiry. See Figure 7.1.

Starter Time: 10 minutes	Before this session students have: 1. Reviewed their inquiry journals. 2. Highlighted what they found interesting. In preparation for this session, have students collect these ideas in one place in their inquiry journal. While they are reviewing their journals, advise them to be thinking about possible inquiry questions. Introduce the idea that making a chart helps you to find ideas that fit together and helps to identify a meaningful direction for your inquiry. In this session, students will chart interesting ideas to help them identify their inquiry question. Model how to develop a cluster chart that builds around similarities and differences and how that raises inquiry questions. (See Figure 7.3)
Worktime Time: 30 minutes Charting may take more than one session Materials: Chart paper Color markers 7.3 Handout Inquiry chart Inquiry journal	Have students organize their ideas in a cluster chart by doing the following: Look for an important idea and write it within a circle. Look for similar ideas and place each in a circle near the first. This group of circles is an idea cluster. When you see an idea that doesn't fit into this idea cluster, start a new circle. Look for similar ideas and build another idea cluster around that idea. Continue until you have three idea clusters. Try to fit lone ideas into one of your idea clusters. You may end up with a few ideas that don't seem to fit in any of the clusters. That's ok. Think about each idea cluster. Form a question (why or how) that represents each idea cluster. Write the question on the chart above the cluster. These are your possible questions for deeper investigation. Circulate among students to help guide where needed.

Figure 7.2 Identify Model Session Plan

Reflection Time: 15 minutes; more time as needed Inquiry circles	Students gather in their inquiry circles and share their cluster charts and questions. Discuss the question: How did charting help them to create questions? Encourage students to share the process they went through and the thinking that helped them arrive at the questions. The students can also discuss the usefulness of the questions they chose with their inquiry circle. Students can then write questions on a chart paper to post in the room and share with the inquiry community.
Notes:	Some students may be ready to identify an inquiry question before others. This can be a mini lesson, with one inquiry circle at a time depending on your time frame and diversity of learners.

Figure 7.2 Identify Model Session Plan (*Continued*)

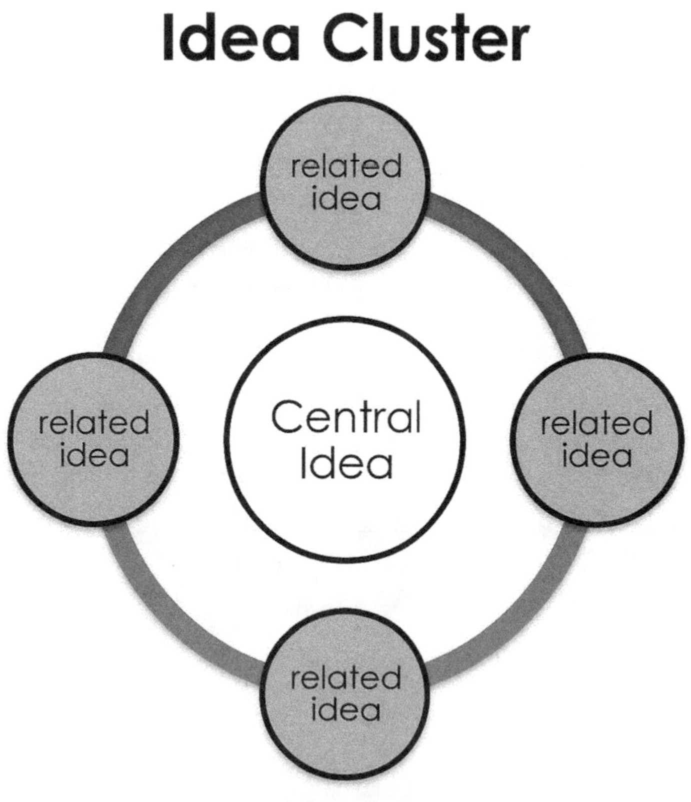

Idea Cluster

Figure 7.3 Idea Cluster Map

MODEL SESSION PLAN

OPEN - IMMERSE - EXPLORE - **IDENTIFY** - GATHER - CREATE- SHARE - EVALUATE

Learning Goals: Pause and ponder and decide direction; use charting to decide and identify an inquiry question
Location: Library or classroom
Team: Whole team

Starter	
Time: 10 minutes	Students will understand that decisions are made based on criteria. Students will list their possible inquiry questions and use the criteria to decide which questions are best suited for deeper investigation.
In preparation for this session, students have:	
Reviewed their inquiry journal. Re-read sources already dipped into.	Connections: Making decisions requires thought. Informed decision-making includes weighing the many factors that play into the decision. Think about the last time you made a decision. Talk to a partner about what decision you made. On what basis did you make that decision? Discuss in whole group one or two examples from students. Talk about what criteria they used to make a decision. Make a link to the criteria they will use for choosing a question to research.
Highlighted what is interesting, and recorded their current thoughts in journal entries. They have also created a list of possible questions for inquiry.	You will be making a decision today. You will decide which inquiry question you will be spending your time investigating further. It's an important decision because your time and effort is important to you. You want to spend your time on something worthwhile.
Students need task card and Criteria to Decide handout.	Introduce Criteria for Deciding handout. Display the four considerations on a screen or poster (see handout). Model use of criteria in a think-aloud session with one student. Cluster chart or a model chart to consider:
	• What am I trying to accomplish?
	• How interested am I in this idea?
	• How much time do I have?
	• What information and resources are available?
	Students will use these criteria to help them decide on the question they wish to pursue.
	Students will have the task card* and handouts* to follow along during the think-aloud session.

Figure 7.4 Identify Model Session Plan

Worktime Time: 30 minutes	Students will use the cluster chart that helped them to identify possible questions. Have students write three possible inquiry questions in their inquiry journal. Ask students to think about the four considerations for deciding on an inquiry question: • What am I trying to accomplish? • How interested am I in this idea? • How much time do I have? • What information and resources are available? The students analyze the top three inquiry questions on their list, using the chart of the criteria to decide. As they consider each question, they will evaluate each based on the four criteria listed in the boxes on the handout. Then the students will prioritize their questions (top, second, and last choices). Have students identify their top choice to discuss with their inquiry circle. This process helps them to read, reflect, and review in order to rethink the ideas that they've already explored to form an inquiry question.
Reflection Time: 15 minutes	Once the students identify their top choice, they will share with their inquiry circle. Encourage students to debate with each other the choices they made. During the debate, each student should provide the inquiry circle with a solid rationale for their choice by explaining the criteria on which their decision was made. Students could use this sentence stem: I chose this question because... (A solid rationale includes most of the elements of the criteria: time, interest, available resources, goal.)
Notes: See task card and handout	May be done in small groups because some students may become ready to identify an inquiry question before others. This can also be facilitated as a mini lesson, with one small group or inquiry circle at a time depending on your time frame and diversity of learners.

Figure 7.4 Identify Model Session Plan (*Continued*)

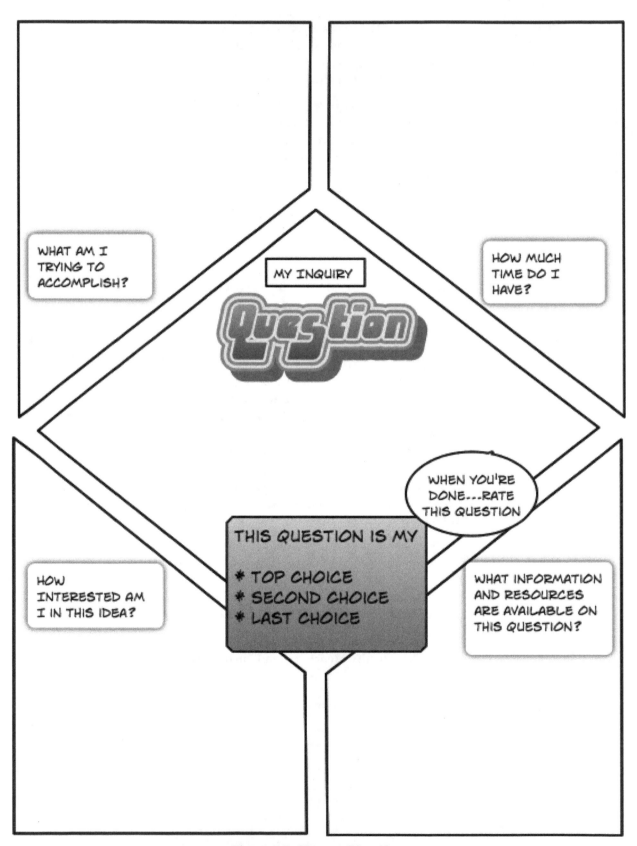

Figure 7.5 Chart to Identify

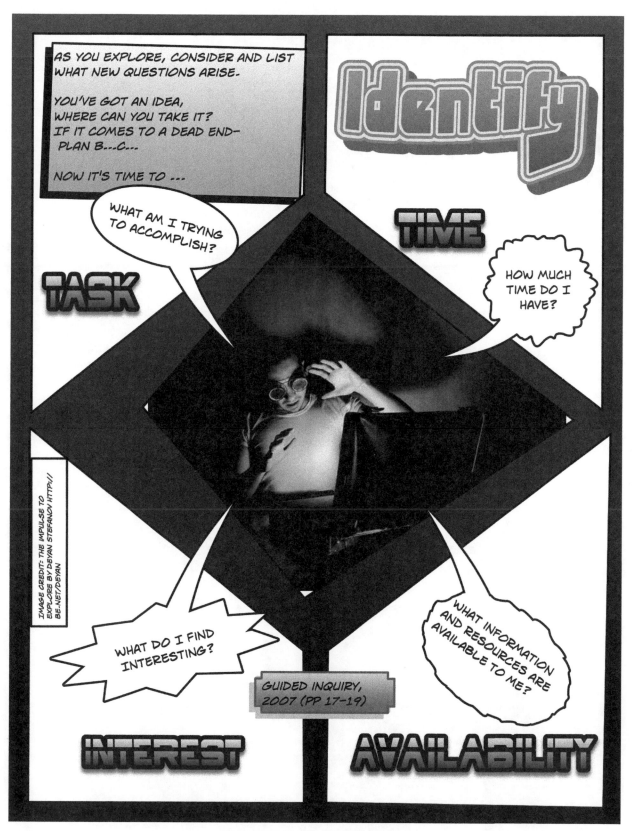

Figure 7.6 Taskcard for Identify

Gather

- **Gather important information**
- **Go broad**
- **Go deep**

8

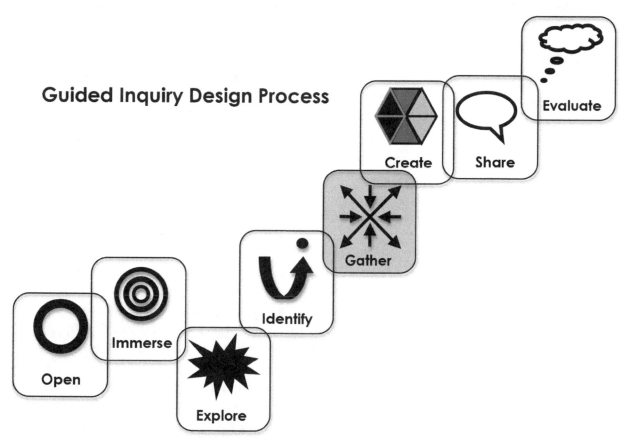

Guided Inquiry Design Process

Open • Immerse • Explore • Identify • Gather • Create • Share • Evaluate

A clearly articulated question gives direction for the Gather phase. Gather sessions are designed to help students collect detailed information from a variety of sources that engages them in learning about their inquiry question. The learning team guides students in locating, evaluating, and using information that leads to deep learning.

The main purpose of the Gather phase is to guide learners to choose what is personally meaningful and compelling about their inquiry question in the information sources they find. The learning team guides students in a structured approach for managing their search. Students "go broad" to find a range of sources that are useful to understand their inquiry question. Students also "go deep" and choose a core of the most useful sources to read closely as they find connections and gain personal understanding.

The Research

Collection Stage of the Information Search Process

In the Collection stage of the Information Search Process (ISP), the task was to gather information pertaining to the focused topic. During this stage, the type of information sought shifted from what is relevant to the general topic to what is pertinent to the focus. A clear focus enabled students to discriminate between general information on the broad topic and specific information pertinent to their focus. A good focus could be adapted and altered while students collected information. Although students kept the focus clearly in mind, they also needed to refine and revise it as they read and took notes. The focus changed somewhat as information was gathered in this stage. When students expected change to take place, they actively sought to refine and adapt their focus through the information they collected. As students gathered information throughout this stage, they continued to learn about their focus. As they read, thoughts were more clearly defined and extended by new information. They took notes on the ideas and facts to build their understanding about the focus. Students who had difficulty collecting information frequently did not have a clear focus in mind. They lacked the structure upon which to build their ideas.

Gather in Guided Inquiry

Gather is designed as a time of comprehensive searching that encompasses locating, evaluating, and using a variety of sources of information to learn about an important focused question. Searching is fun and absorbing and has become a popular pastime for people of all ages. Searching is a common way to inquire about everyday questions in all walks of life. Inquiry is a naturally enjoyable part of our lives that is brought into schools through Guided Inquiry. Young children welcome a call to "go find out." Most older children and teens find searching interesting and enjoyable. In Identify, students take the time to choose a question of high interest to them that propels them into a flow of intriguing searching. Although this is the time in the inquiry process to get down to the nitty-gritty of gathering information, the team will want to be sure to highlight the fun part of searching and gathering.

Thoughts about the inquiry question change as information is gathered. Students need to be receptive to learning as they gather information. Often they are not seeking an answer but rather a deeper picture or understanding of their question. The learning team helps students to learn that inquiry is about addressing a meaningful inquiry question and gaining deep understanding, not simply getting a right answer.

The team designs a concepts approach to information literacy by introducing skills and strategies at the time students need to put them to use in the inquiry process. The school librarian is the expert in teaching and modeling search strategies that are integrated into the inquiry process to build competency in grades pre-K through secondary school. Guided Inquiry is designed to enable students to learn search strategies that are transferable to a wide range of situations inside and outside of school.

Gather is designed to provide students some structures for managing their information searching and collecting. The learning team introduces inquiry journals and inquiry logs in the early stages of the inquiry process that are used as management tools in the Gather phase. Students have been introduced to these inquiry tools for Explore and are familiar with using them by the time they have reached the Gather phase. Students who have used these inquiry tools through the early grades will be comfortable applying them in the middle and secondary grades as they move into more sophisticated Gather phases in their inquiry learning.

Go Broad: A Comprehensive Search on Inquiry Question

The school librarian leads the learning team in guiding students to see the distinct difference between Gather strategies used at this point in the inquiry process and Explore strategies used earlier in the inquiry process. Gather is a systematic approach to locating a variety of sources to gather information that is pertinent to an inquiry question. A broad comprehensive search is possible because the question sets the boundaries. In Gather, going broad is framed by the inquiry question. Searching and gathering may be thought of as a journey that creates a path or trail from one source to another. Students use their inquiry log to track the journey.

Information gathering involves a series of choices of what to use, what might be useful, and what not to use. It is helpful to point out to students that they will need to make "yes or no" choices throughout this phase of inquiry. Their inquiry logs are a complete record of the citations of sources they have chosen as useful in Gather. As they go broad in a comprehensive search, they will continue to add the sources that they evaluate as most useful. At this point, they concentrate on choosing the most important, interesting, high-quality sources of information about their inquiry question (Kuhlthau, Maniotes & Caspari, 2007, p. 79).

The Extended Team in Gather

Youth and children's librarians and reference librarians at the public library are valuable experts to add to the extended team for the Gather phase. Additional resources in the public library can enhance the inquiry for your students. The school librarian can contact the public librarians to introduce the project and arrange a meeting with the learning team. As extended team members, public librarians can design a learning experience around a visit to the public library, either with the whole group or to prepare for individual student visits. This meeting may happen in person, on the phone, via Skype, or email. Inclusion of public librarians in this planning ensures a cohesive match between learning goals and resources.

Depending on the subject of the inquiry, museum exhibits, online collections, academic libraries, and archives may also be added by the extended team at this time. Academic libraries found at universities and archives may be appropriate depending on the age of the student and the sophistication of the inquiry. Often, museums and archives provide access to specific resources such as historical photographs, objects, or ephemera that are enriching to the inquiry and otherwise unavailable. Museums may have a digital collection that can be searched, and they may provide search tools on their web site and even provide information that links the objects in their collection to specific learning standards. Many museums, historical societies, and archives make their collections available digitally. However, often this material is not digitized and is still only accessible through a scheduled appointment through the archivist or librarian at the site. Museum educators at the site can be a valuable go-between to help schedule a session as well as teach about how to glean information from primary sources and objects. At this point, it may be that only one of the inquiry circles will visit a particular site that has information pertinent to their aspect of the inquiry. It is especially appropriate for high school students to have guided experiences in small groups with special collections such as these.

Evaluate to Make Good Choices

Information literacy is embedded in the work of the Gather phase. The school librarian leads the team in teaching and guiding students in evaluating information sources to make good choices. Evaluation criteria of expertise, accuracy, currency, perspective, and quality are introduced as ways to judge the value of sources. Students think about these criteria by asking guided questions. For more on the evaluation criteria see Kuhlthau, Maniotes & Caspari, 2007, p. 85.

Evaluation criteria help students to choose good sources in their broad comprehensive information search and to go deeper in order to choose important information within the sources for learning about their inquiry question. Going broad and going deep are closely connected in Gather. The objective of going broad is to choose a core of quality sources for going deep to address the inquiry question.

Go Deep: Learning from Information Within Sources

Students need to choose a few core sources and to choose what information to use within those sources. They will need to go deep into these core sources to choose information that helps them to learn more about their question. Going deep in Gather involves choosing several high-quality sources that address their inquiry question in interesting, thought-provoking ways. Most students will need guidance in choosing these core sources from the useful sources they have recorded in their inquiry log. Going deep involves choosing specific information within the core sources to write about in the inquiry journal.

A different kind of reading takes place during the Gather phase than during the Explore phase. In Gather, by close reading and engaging deeply with texts and sources, students gain a clear picture and thorough understanding of their question. Their reading leads them to important facts and ideas that they write about in their inquiry journal. They learn to distinguish important facts and big ideas from insignificant facts and minor details that can distract and bog down their learning. They may continue to uncover opposing points of view, confusing ideas, and facts that don't fit together smoothly. But now they are able to work through these conflicting ideas within the context of their inquiry question. The team is aware when students need extra help to resolve these conflicts. Conferencing with students is a good way to monitor individual progress during Gather. Deep reading and reflection lead to making connections, interpreting, and learning in order to create an inquiry product to share.

Going deep calls for the study mode of Gather, rather than the relaxing mode of Explore. In the study mode, students sit at tables or desks where they have a surface to lay out materials, take notes, or use a computer. The study mode is more conducive to the work of the Gather phase of the inquiry process.

Gathering Important Information

Students need to be able to choose the important information and ideas in their core sources that address their inquiry question. Determining importance is a vital ability in learning from these information sources. Students of all ages often find it difficult to choose what is most important from insignificant details and unimportant facts. They can easily get bogged down attempting to copy down everything from a text. They need to learn how to choose what to use and to feel confident in their choices.

What students choose to summarize as important from a passage will vary. In this way, choosing important information shows their personal learning. The team can guide them to reread if they have missed essential points, but it is necessary that students feel free to write about what they actually remember as important in the text. Their ability to draw out important ideas will improve with repeated practice along with their comprehension to interpret a text.

Determining importance is one of the most difficult strategies to teach students. This exercise helps students to learn to think about what they have read and to draw out what is important rather than to just copy the author's words. It also helps them to retain what they have learned. When the exercise is repeated throughout the Gather phase of the inquiry process with various texts as they "go deep," it can be developed into a valuable inquiry habit.

Instructions for this task in modeling the strategy could be, "After reading something important related to your question, close the book and think about what you have read. Then write what you recall in your inquiry journal (Figure 8.1). It is important to close the book when you write your summary and to write from what you remember as important from what you read. Your writing will need to follow shortly after you have read the passage. Then some time later, read what you have written and add anything else you remember as important. You may need to go back to check on some facts." At this point, students can share and discuss what they have written in their inquiry journals in conversations in their inquiry circles. This exercise can be used following the reading of a text or following an experience such as a video, audio, expert presentation, a museum exhibit, or field excursion.

The advantage of this go deep practice is that it breaks the habit of copying a text word for word. It helps students to rely on their own impression of what is important in a text and gives them a strategy for making choices of importance. Members of the learning team may decide to conduct individual conferences with some students at this phase to give additional guidance and support as they learn new skills and habits.

Citing, Quoting, and Paraphrasing

Students' inquiry journals have their detailed notes of facts and ideas they chose as most useful and important from their core sources. Being able to determine importance is essential for taking notes from these information sources. Students use inquiry journals for summarizing, paraphrasing, quoting, and interpreting the information they gather. They include their thoughts and interpretations of how this information helps them understand their inquiry question.

INQUIRY JOURNAL: GO DEEP

This inquiry journal exercise will help you to write about the important ideas you find when you Go Deep. This helps you to see what you have learned from your reading and to write about what is important to you.

After reading something important related to your question, close the book and think about what you have read.	**Read and think**
Write what you recall in your inquiry journal. It is important to close the book when you write your journal entry and to write from what you remember was important.	**Recall and write**
Some time later, read what you have written and add anything else you remember as important. Now you may want to go back to check on some facts.	**Review and add**
Think about what you have written and respond with your own ideas.	**Think and respond**

Figure 8.1 Gather Inquiry Journal: Go Deep

Some teachers say that they don't assign research because students just copy from the Internet. Students need to use information and ideas in all aspects of their everyday lives. Research is more important than ever. It is no longer just an academic skill; it is a life skill. Not assigning research in schools is not the answer or even an option. Unfortunately, some of these teachers equate research papers with inquiry. Rethinking the research assignment is essential. That's what Guided Inquiry does.

Ethical use of information is important throughout the Guided Inquiry process, and the Gather phase is where the requirement for ethical use of information is most important. Learners must present their own ideas and cite the ideas they have borrowed from others. In order to paraphrase, students need to know words that can be used in place of the author's words. Young children can learn to paraphrase and can simultaneously learn that a wide vocabulary can help them to paraphrase texts for inquiry. Making lists or thesaurus-type word walls with multiple words under a core word will build the habit students need to put things into their own words. This is a critical skill for the technological information environment. The Guided Inquiry team coaches students in ethical use of information throughout the process from Open to Create. Students learn that plagiarism is not clever, acceptable, or wise. They learn how to do their own work, deepen their own learning, and create an innovative way to share what they have learned.

The learning team guides students in making choices that will shape the story they want to tell about what they are learning about the inquiry question. Students need to learn the difference between quoting, paraphrasing, and interpreting and how to cite the source in each case. Young children can choose when "it's good to use the author's words and when it's better to use your own." And they can learn to note which is which. Older students need to learn to value their own way of expressing an idea and be diligent about giving the originator of works credit through proper citation. Students use inquiry journals for summarizing, paraphrasing, quoting, and interpreting the information they gather. They include their thoughts and interpretations of the information they are gathering.

Students may be guided to color code each of these different types of writing and to highlight places in their journals where they are expressing their own ideas or interpretations. It will be important for them to distinguish their own ideas and wording from quotes or paraphrasing when they create and share the product of the inquiry.

Decide What is Enough

Students need to learn how to decide what is enough. Enough is an important information literacy concept in light of the extraordinary increase in access to information provided by each new technology. The team will want students to consider how to know when you have enough and to learn ways to tell what is enough. Of course, one way is when the deadline is approaching. But the learning team can guide students to learn more authentic ways of determining that an inquiry is coming to a close.

An authentic way to decide is to ask some questions that stimulate thinking about enough. For instance, the team may ask students the following questions as prompts for journal writing: What have you learned about your inquiry question? What surprises you that you didn't expect? What's the big idea behind the facts you are gathering? The team will look for evidence that students are ready to go beyond facts to interpret meaning and extend into their own lives. A good way to have students decide is to ask them, "Do you have enough to tell the story of what you have learned?"

At the close of Gather, the learning team may want to introduce students to a summary search. Conducting a summary search is helpful for middle school and secondary school students when they want to be sure they have not overlooked significant sources, verify a citation of a source they used, or confirm a particular fact or idea.

The Gather phase is the time to talk about the number of sources that are needed and how much detail to go into to communicate what they have learned. This is where these decisions fit into the process of learning, rather than at the opening when the announcement of the requirements and mechanics detracts from the inviting ideas that should drive the inquiry. Setting the parameters of what is enough from the perspective of the learning team and the students is important. The students and team need to come to an understanding of what is enough to meet the learning goals of the inquiry unit. At this point, the mechanics of the inquiry become important. Students will need to have authentic ways to decide with the learning team on the grading rubric of the project. This is a good time to turn attention to the product, the format, and how students will be graded.

Assessing to Guide Gathering

Inquiry journals are data sources for assessing student learning in Gather. Journals are a valuable formative assessment tool for alerting the learning team when students need guidance throughout this stage. The learning team will need to read and respond to the inquiry journals on a regular basis. They will need to check students' journals frequently to provide timely guidance that is tailored to specific learning needs. For instance, some students may indicate a need for extra help in distinguishing between important ideas and minor details. Perhaps the journals show that the whole group can benefit from instruction on using primary source material to develop a deeper first-hand experience and heighten engagement and interest. Inquiry journals provide insight into what students are thinking, doing and, feeling that gives the learning team an opportunity to target individual and group guidance to meet specific learning needs at the time when most helpful.

What is the Team Doing?

The learning team uses modeling, listening, and encouraging to foster third space in inquiry learning. In the Gather phase, the team models information literacy skills for locating sources and evaluating techniques for choosing sources. The team listens to students for evidence of synthesis and interpretation of ideas. They encourage students to take an original perspective on the topic as they paraphrase and extend ideas from their search.

Modeling

The school librarian models search strategies for locating sources and for evaluating techniques to use in order to choose good sources by applying criteria of expertise, accuracy, currency, perspective, and quality. They model how to address a meaningful inquiry question and gain deep understanding, not simply getting a right answer. The team needs to be alert to when students need extra help to resolve these conflicts. The team models the way that inquiry journals are used in Gather for taking detailed notes on information specifically related to the inquiry question and for summarizing, paraphrasing, quoting, and interpreting the information.

Listening

The team listens to students' explanations of determining importance to be sure they are able to choose big ideas and are not getting bogged down in insignificant facts and unimportant details. At the end of Gather, the team listens for evidence that students are ready to go beyond facts to interpret meaning and extend into their own lives by having students respond to the question, do you have enough to tell the story of what you have learned?

Encouraging

The learning team encourages students to do their own original thinking about their inquiry question and to value the passages in the inquiry journal where they are summarizing, paraphrasing, interpreting, and extending. Students are also encouraged to show the development of their thinking and learning and to relate that learning to their own lives.

Assessing

Inquiry logs are a quick and easy data source for monitoring when students need help finding quality sources or different media formats or materials that are better matched to students' age and developmental level. Inquiry journals are data sources for alerting the learning team when students need help throughout this phase and provide timely guidance that is tailored to specific learning needs. Conferences with students in conjunction with these other tools help the team guide learning and keep a pulse on where students are in the inquiry process and in their progress as students make meaning and come to deeper understandings.

What is the Learner Doing?

During Gather, students use inquiry tools to track sources, gather useful information, and extend learning through collaborations in the inquiry community.

Inquiry Log for Tracking Most Useful Sources

The inquiry log can be in either paper or digital format. Students started their inquiry logs in the Explore phase and found sources of citations from their exploratory search that may be useful. The record of full citations should be in the format recommended by your school. Many schools use the Modern Language Association format for citations. You will need to teach your students how to follow correct citation format in Explore and continue to model that format in Gather. Although students often can simply cut and paste this information, citing sources is an important part of responsible citizenry in the information age. A simple version of a citation may be introduced to young children, and a more official format introduced in upper elementary and middle school. It is important that students form the habit of acknowledging an author's work in their early encounters with inquiry.

INQUIRY LOG

Use this inquiry log from the Explore stage through the Create stage.

	Explore	**Gather**
Track your choices through the inquiry.	As you explore, check the box if you might use the source for your inquiry. ✔ "Maybe"	As you gather, check the box if you will use the source for your inquiry. ✔ "Use it"
Track the reading strategies you use.	As you explore, place an **x** after the sources you dipped in to.	As you gather, mark an ***** after the core sources you read deeply.

Cite all your sources.

	Source Citation	**Maybe ✔** **Dip in x**	**Notes:** **What makes it useful?**	**Use it ✔** **Go deep ***
1				
2				
3				
4				
5				
6				
7				
8				
9				
10				

Figure 8.2 Inquiry Log

Inquiry logs are data sources for assessing student learning in Gather (Figure 8.2). The school librarian takes the lead in checking the inquiry logs frequently to determine when students need help finding quality sources. Entries in logs may indicate a need for help in finding sources in different media formats to broaden student experience or match learning styles. Logs may indicate a need for materials that are better matched to students' age and developmental level. In addition, the inquiry logs may show a need for help with the mechanics of citing the sources. Inquiry logs are a valuable quick and easy formative assessment tool for alerting the team of the kind of guidance students need throughout the Gather phase.

Students check the "Use it" column during Gather once they have decided that a source is most useful for learning about their inquiry question and worth including in their final list of references. A check here indicates a learning decision. From this list of most useful sources, they choose a few core sources to go deep.

Inquiry Journals for Gathering Useful Information

The ISP shows that students become more interested in their research the further they get into their investigation. A good inquiry question often takes on a life of its own, with students thinking about the ideas they are uncovering far beyond scheduled inquiry sessions as the momentum of inquiry takes hold and students get into the flow. "Stop and jot" is a good way to capture these ideas.

During Gather, the learning team can recommend that students keep their inquiry journal handy so that they can stop and jot down ideas when they occur to them and return to these ideas during scheduled inquiry sessions. Stop and jot is a good way to think about this spontaneous kind of journaling that captures ideas before they slip away. The teaching team can instruct students, "Get in the habit when a good idea comes to you to jot it down in your journal. Everyone has flashes of insight and often these happen when you are thinking about something else. Stop and jot is a good way to capture flashes of insight."

Organizing inquiry journals to incorporate these different kinds of notes is an important part of guiding learners in Gather. The inquiry journal is an original composing instrument that shows learning over the course of the inquiry process. Students need to have a clear understanding that this is their original work. It is not necessary to get it "perfect." However, it is important to show their own original thinking about the inquiry question that they have identified to investigate and learn about. The most valued passages in the inquiry journal are their summarizing, paraphrasing, interpreting, and extending, which show the development of their thinking and learning and how they relate that learning to their own lives.

Inquiry journals are used for gathering information specifically related to the inquiry question. As students go deep into a core of the most useful sources, they use their inquiry journals for summarizing, paraphrasing, quoting, and interpreting information within these sources. They include their thoughts and reflections of the information and ideas they are gathering. Students have their inquiry journals available so they can stop and jot down ideas.

Students are guided to go beyond reporting on facts and to interpret the meaning of the facts and incorporate their own ideas about what they have found. All learners will need to apply summarizing skills in their creations. Summarizing is a difficult skill that requires strategies and practice. Learners need to form habits of not telling all but telling what is most important. They need to recognize that there is not one main idea or one right answer for all. Guided Inquiry allows students to have a point of view and an opinion, substantiated by information. They form the habit

MODEL SESSION PLAN

OPEN - IMMERSE - EXPLORE - IDENTIFY - **GATHER** - CREATE- SHARE - EVALUATE

Learning Goals: Go deep, gather important information
Location: School library
Team: Learning team

This Gather session helps students gain an understanding of going deep into a text to find what is important to record and write about in their inquiry journal and to track in their inquiry log.

Starter Time: 15 minutes Inquiry log	Before this session, students go broad to find a range of sources that are useful to understand their inquiry question. From the sources they have recorded in their inquiry log, they select and star several core sources to go deep into to address their inquiry question. This is an introduction to going deep during Gather. This session is geared around guiding students to go deep and determine importance related to a well-formed question. Introduce go deep. Model how to go deep by thinking aloud through a text. For example, "My question is, what are the possible causes of global warming? I am reading to find out more about global warming and finding some controversy about its possible causes." Read aloud a passage regarding this controversy and model the decision-making process for determining what is important and what ideas of my own I want to include by responding to the following questions: • What do I think is most important in this passage? • How would I summarize what is most important? • What might I quote directly? • What ideas, connections, and interpretations does it raise for me? Have the questions on display during the session. Other sessions—Model how to take notes from the text responding to these questions. Model how to choose what's important for addressing the question; to summarize these ideas; to highlight quotes; to add their own ideas, connections, and interpretations; and to record all in their inquiry journals.

Figure 8.3 Gather Model Session Plan

Worktime Time: 20–30 minutes Inquiry journal	In preparation for the worktime, have each inquiry circle select a common text for deep reading from the core sources chosen in their inquiry logs from their broad searches. Ask the students to read the text and write in their inquiry journals about what they find important related to their inquiry question. Although each inquiry circle has the same general topic, each student has a somewhat different inquiry question related to the general topic. Each student will pull out different information and make different connections from this same text. As they read, have them use their inquiry journals to document importance, noting any of their own ideas that occur to them at the time. Remind them to think about the four questions to help them determine importance and decide what to summarize or quote and to add their own ideas, connections, and interpretations.
Reflection Time: 20 minutes Inquiry circles Inquiry journals Inquiry logs	Have students gather in their inquiry circles to summarize what they found important and why it is important for addressing their question. Have them add their own thoughts to begin building connections and deeper meaning. As they share and discuss with their inquiry circle, guide students to realize that what each person gathers is related to their question and is different from the others, even within the same text, because the inquiry questions are different. At the close of the session, have each student discuss other sources in their inquiry logs that they have chosen to go deep into in the coming sessions and why they have chosen the source.
Notes: The entries in the inquiry log and inquiry journal are data sources for assessment.	After this session, students go deep into the core sources they have chosen and write in their journals about what they find important for addressing their inquiry question. Their writing includes notes and summaries of important ideas with their own reactions, interpretations, and connections. They also highlight any quotations they may use. In this phase, continual guidance by the learning team is needed to ensure that students understand the work of gathering and begin to discover insights to construct a story about what they are finding. As students talk about important ideas and concepts they are reading about with their inquiry circles, they work together to support meaning-making.

Figure 8.3 Gather Model Session Plan (*Continued*)

of making a case by telling what they think about what they have learned. They are encouraged to express their thoughts and urged to put their own ideas into their creations.

There is a close relationship between summarizing and interpreting. In Guided Inquiry, students use recall, summarize, paraphrase, and extend to promote deep thinking throughout the phases of the inquiry process. These writings, which are recorded in their inquiry journals, prepare them for interpreting in the Create phase. Writing to communicate is a primary strategy for creating in Guided Inquiry. Through writing, students clarify their ideas and define and synthesize their understanding while articulating their thoughts for others.

Inquiry Community

Students continue to gather information to address their inquiry question within their inquiry community. They are provided whole-group instruction in mini-lessons on search strategies and source highlights at the time of need. They work individually in an inquiry environment surrounded and supported by their inquiry community.

Inquiry Circles

The Gather phase doesn't need to be an isolated, individual experience in order for each student to construct their own personal understanding of his or her inquiry question. At times students work on their own and at other times in their inquiry circles. For many students, collaborative work settings are more conducive to concentrating and keeping on task.

In the following example, elementary school students in an inquiry community are working in inquiry circles to find important information about their inquiry question from a variety of sources. They are working in a collaborative study mode. The school librarian has organized a digital library of selected sources for their inquiry unit. The students have been using the digital library to go broad to find useful sources. They have selected a few core sources to go deep together in a collaborative study mode.

The students are working collaboratively in inquiry circles on laptops at tables. Each circle is reading and reflecting on the core sources they have chosen from the inquiry unit digital library for addressing their inquiry questions. In each circle, one student is writing notes for the group while others read and discuss to determine big ideas. In one circle, a student pulls up a map and shows it to her circle members to check on the location of an important event. In another circle, students are mulling over two web sites that seem to have conflicting information. In a third circle, students are discussing which facts they will need to explain and support the big ideas that are emerging. In this way, collaboration in inquiry circles is helping these students to check on facts to get a clearer picture, work through confusing conflicts, and choose what is important from minor details.

Well-timed collaborative study sessions combined with individual work sessions help students think and learn about the information and ideas they are gathering. The learning team will need to be alert to when the collaborative study mode is most beneficial for supporting student learning during the Gather phase. Inquiry circles provide a collaborative study mode that many students find conducive to concentrating and keeping on task, particularly when distinguishing between important information and insignificant details. Conversations in inquiry circles help students make connections among ideas and facts and to interpret and synthesize the information they gather to address their inquiry question. In Gather, inquiry circle conversations help students identify gaps in their thinking and construct meaningful learning.

Although Inquiry circles were flexible in Immerse and Explore, they are now designed so that the students are purposely grouped around the content of their inquiry question. Students who are pursuing questions around the same subtopic on the larger theme are grouped together. This makes the collaborative environment of inquiry circles even richer. Students come to the inquiry circles to share their notes and ideas and share sources with one another. They have deeper discussions about their topic than they can with the entire community because of their common interest and information. Inquiry circles advance into this type of collaboration during Gather. When students are expected to have intelligent conversations in the circles, they can offer each other divergent perspectives and the circle can provide a space for debating perspectives and ideas. In this way, the circles enrich the learning in profound ways as students co-construct understandings and problem-solve around conflicting information.

Ideas for Gather Sessions

In Gather, there are many concepts to introduce, teach, model and practice (see Figure 8.2). These sessions must be purposefully designed to match the learners' information needs, knowledge, and ability. The team designs sessions that guide students to learn how to apply search strategies, conduct a comprehensive search, and use a wide range of sources in a variety of media. Criteria are introduced for evaluating different types of sources as well as a structure for managing the gathering of useful information.

Key strategies for finding important information in core sources, determining importance, paraphrasing, and quoting are introduced, modeled, and practiced. Mini-lessons center on when to quote and when to paraphrase, what to include in a summary, how to interpret, and how to extend what is in the text.

The team guides individuals through conferences and provides advice on what to quote and paraphrase when needed. They create a quiet space for concentration and a collaborative environment for construction. The team guides students in finding paths through core sources for specific information about questions and generally ensures an environment for going beyond fact-finding to interpreting and extending to the students' world.

What's Next? Create

Gather is a time of concentrated searching and intense learning that prepares students for the Create phase of the inquiry process. At the close of Gather, students have gained a deep understanding of their inquiry question. They have quoted, paraphrased, interpreted, and extended the information they have gathered to tell the story of what they have learned and are ready to create a way to share that learning with their inquiry community and other audiences.

PAIR SHARE PROTOCOL

Pair Share Protocol Prompts	Choosing and Summarizing Important Information
As you review your journal, highlight the most important ideas you gathered about your inquiry question.	Three most important ideas about my question . . .
Write about what these ideas show you about your inquiry question.	These ideas show me that . . .
Read over what you have written and write what you would like to tell someone else about.	I would like to tell about . . .
Pair Share Partner A: Shares. Partner B: Listens and takes notes. Partner B: Shares Partner A: Listens and takes notes.	Share with your partner and take notes. Telling helps to clarify your ideas about what is important and helps you summarize the important ideas about your inquiry question.
Partners exchange notes.	Your partner's notes on what you share can help you summarize the important ideas and give you insight into how these ideas fit together.
Reflect on what you found important and how you described it to your partner. Think about possible connections between these important ideas.	Now write a summary in your inquiry journal of the most important ideas and add connections you see between these ideas.

Figure 8.4 Gather Pair Share Protocol

Create

- **Reflect on learning**
- **Go beyond facts to make meaning**
- **Create to communicate**

9

Guided Inquiry Design Process

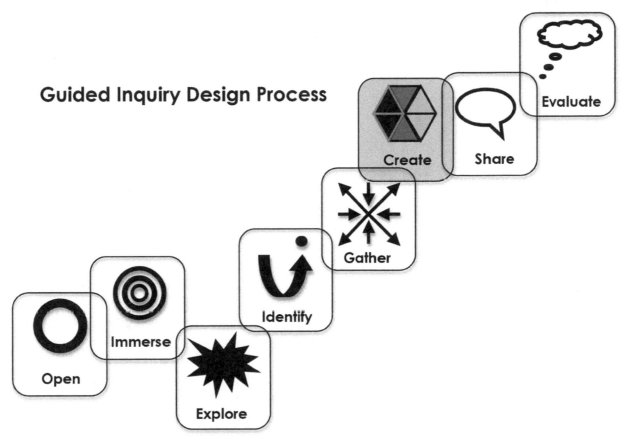

After students have gathered enough information to construct their own understandings, they are ready to organize their learning into a creative presentation in the Create phase. Creating a way to communicate what they have learned about their inquiry helps students to articulate what is important about the subject and requires them to integrate the ideas more firmly into a deep understanding. The learning team guides students to go beyond simple fact-finding and reporting and to summarize, interpret, and extend the meaning of what they have learned and to create a way to share their learning.

Create sessions are designed to guide students to reflect on all they have learned about their inquiry question, construct their own understanding, and decide what type of presentation will best represent their engaging ideas, controversies, and theories, which were generated through the inquiry, for a particular audience. The learning team guides students in creating a meaningful, interesting, clearly articulated, well-documented presentation that tells the story of what they have learned in the inquiry process.

The Research

Presentation Stage of the Information Search Process

In the Presentation stage of the Information Search Process (ISP), the task was to complete the search and prepare to present the findings, usually as a written paper, sometimes accompanied by an oral or visual presentation or a combination of all of these. When students entered the last stage of the ISP, most of their library research had been completed. Some students made a final summary search to be sure they had not overlooked significant sources, verify a citation of a source they had used, or confirm a particular fact or idea. However, most searching had been finished by this stage. Notes taken in the Collection stage were reread to identify main points around which to organize related information. In this way, students built a framework for presenting their findings about their focus of the topic.

Students had a sense of relief after the search was complete. However, the Presentation stage marked the beginning of the writing process, which presented another set of challenges. Students who had constructed their ideas as they collected information were prepared for writing and presenting and often expressed a sense of accomplishment and satisfaction. Students who had not formed a focus, had rushed through their search, or, for some other reason, had not developed their thoughts through the ISP often felt disappointed at this point. These studies showed that students who had not formed a clear focus in the ISP had difficulty writing their papers. A clear focus provided not only a frame for collecting information, it also provided a frame for organizing and writing the presentation. Writing blocks evident in the Presentation stage of the ISP showed the importance of intervention for constructing learning throughout the inquiry process and the necessity for guidance in creating a way to share that learning with others.

Guided Inquiry separates the ISP stage of Presentation into two phases: Create and Share. Creating in Guided Inquiry involves guidance for going beyond facts to interpreting meaning to share what has been learned using a variety of media.

Create in Guided Inquiry

The Guided Inquiry Design Framework prepares students for this moment. Now they are ready to create and share what they have learned through the inquiry process. The previous chapters have outlined the Guided Inquiry Design Framework that guides in the research process, which precedes the creative process of writing. In the earlier phases, students built ideas and information that they can now use. This chapter provides strategies to design ways to guide students as they synthesize their ideas and pull it all together to share in the inquiry community. Create is exciting and fun but it requires a struggle. Pulling together a lot of ideas and finding a way to tell a complex story takes time, reflection, and thoughtful guidance. Create in the Design Framework offers strategies to guide students to persist through the challenges of creating.

Creating an inquiry product is a demonstration of learning and not simply a closing activity. The learning team guides students to reflect on all they have learned about their inquiry questions, interpret and extend their ideas and reconnect into their own life, and create to communicate the knowledge and insights they gained throughout the inquiry process. The learning team introduces strategies for creating and provides assistance for students to experience a positive outcome when they share what they have learned in the inquiry process.

Reflect on Learning

The main task in Create is to synthesize all the ideas and pull together a personal perspective on the inquiry question. Before students begin to synthesize ideas, Create sessions are designed to help students reflect on the information and ideas they have accumulated in their inquiry journals. Charting is an essential tool in the Create phase. Inquiry charts pull disparate ideas together and help reveal themes in the inquiry journals. As Roam (2008) explains in *The Back of the Napkin,* visual thinking is made up of four steps: first we look, next we see, and then we imagine and show.

This is a simple, useful approach to designing the Create phase of Guided Inquiry. When students are ready to create, the learning team guides them to survey their journal entries and *look* at what they have. They should have a wide range of entries on a variety of sources, and taking a look at it all is not an easy task. Roam suggests that we "lay everything out where we can look at it" (p. 63). Students can take everything they have and literally lay it out and look at what they have with the purpose of looking for things that go together and things that don't seem to fit. From that initial look, students begin to *see* ideas and make connections. However, this first step is designed to be left open for just looking around and reflecting on what is there. The next section turns to interpreting and synthesizing where looking becomes seeing.

Going Beyond Facts to Interpret and Extend

Once students have taken time to reflect on all that they have, they begin to *see*. Students can begin to see even more clearly as they chart their ideas and information. Charting enables them to organize a large amount of information in a compact way. Themes arise, patterns emerge, and connections come to the surface. Here is where they go beyond facts and information to interpret what the information means. In Identify, students chose a question to pursue that framed their search through the Gather phase of the inquiry process. Their inquiry question continues to frame their thinking in the Create phase as they interpret the information they have gathered for meaningful connections.

The third step is to *imagine*. Once an inquiry chart is developed out of all the information, the team guides the students to ask, "so what?" This is when students begin to extend their understanding into their own lives. They think of the world and relevance of the idea to themselves and others. Charting is a useful tool in the prewriting process. Once students have considered "so what", they can begin drafting and composing to Create.

One way to approach charting is to determine whether the inquiry question is a who, what, where, why, or how question. Roam (2008) explains that for each kind of question there is a particular way to visualize the information. A *what* or *who* question is visualized by describing to create a portrait. Listing details and symbolic charting of ideas can be used for analysis and description. With *how-many* questions, graphs and comparison charts work well. *Where* questions can be charted with maps, concept maps, diagrams, and drawings of places, networks, and relationships. *When* questions require timelines. Multiple events can be compared with overlapping timelines. Cyclical events such as life processes can be charted with a circular form. Timelines help put things into perspective in a larger frame of time or in conjunction with other events. *How* questions are explored to show how one thing influences another, show relationships, and starting and stopping points. Flowcharts help to problem-solve. Flowcharts are visual representations that define problems and show possible solutions to draw conclusions. *Why* questions indicate a comparison. Using a graphic along two axes can help students examine the way two things work together.

Create sessions are designed to guide students in charting to interpret all the information they have. There are many ways to chart ideas and Roam's book provides a useful starting place. When computers are readily available to students, another tool for charting is the gallery in Microsoft Word. The team can guide students to browse the Smart Art Graphics gallery for a chart that matches their information and ideas. The sidebar describes the kind of information and relationship the chart portrays applying the categories list: process, cycle, hierarchy, relationship, matrix, and pyramid. Most importantly, Create sessions are designed to guide students to a charting tool that can help them synthesize the ideas in a useful way in order to address their inquiry question.

Every student may not be ready to begin to Create at the same time or complete the creations at the same time. Some flexibility will need to be designed into the Create time frame. Recognize that at times deadlines will need to be adjusted to provide for varying pace, of course within reason. A clear deadline is a healthy closure point as long as it takes into account the reality of different student's progress in the Guided Inquiry learning process. Students who are farther along in their process may present to their classmates before the others have completed creating their presentations. They may then be available to give advice or help to the other students or to go further with their investigations based on feedback and questions generated during their presentation. This group editing process is a valuable aspect of inquiry, demonstrating that an inquiry can always continue further, but also that each project must come to a point of closure as well.

Create to Communicate

In Guided Inquiry, every creation begins with writing. As we explained in *Guided Inquiry: Learning in the 21st Century*:

The inquiry process is the process of getting ideas from new information to write about. The inquiry process is closely related to the writing process as described in Janet Emig's (1971) groundbreaking research. It is the *prewriting* stage of the writing process when students are exploring and formulating ideas. Writing blocks are actually thinking blocks where thoughts haven't been sufficiently formed to present ideas. The inquiry process precedes the writing process to prepare students for writing by giving them something to talk about and in turn write about. It is during the inquiry process that students build constructs for writing, composing, and creating. (Kuhlthau, Maniotes, Caspari 2007, p. 22)

Create in Guided Inquiry develops students sense of ownership, expertise, and pride in their learning. The end products tell the stories of what they have learned using written, spoken and visual presentation. Students create ways that open up multiple intelligences by combining the arts, visual, music, dance, and drama with a wide variety of technologies, formats, and media. Their creative products expand the scope and content of the curriculum.

Sometimes the team decides on one type of format for creating for a very specific purpose and all students are required to apply that format. For example, in one school the team connected with a noted local videographer who helped students create videos that showcased the content they were studying. Because these students had the unique opportunity to learn a new skill and apply their learning in video format, they were all required to use the same format. Writing was an important part of this production. They created storyboards that were developed into scripts for the videos.

Other times, students have a choice in what format to use. The learning team guides students to navigate the choices and supports them in pairing the content with just the right format for sharing. The team designs structures for making those decisions. Too many choices can be overwhelming no matter how strong their content knowledge has become through the inquiry process.

In another example, students worked with the school librarian, a third grade teacher, and a science specialist to create a shadow puppet show for preschool students who were exploring shadow and light. The art teacher was included as an extended team member at the Create phase. The third graders had been conducting inquiry about the sun and moon and how shadows are formed by objects as they block a light source. The pre-K students were exploring the same idea at a simpler level. In this example, the third graders worked with the core learning team and the art teacher over several sessions to create a shadow puppet show for the pre-K students.

Creating a puppet show included many discrete and important tasks: reflect on the learning, develop the story, write the script, and create puppets and scenery. The students knew that they needed to show through the action of the puppets, the science that they had been learning about. Using the shadow puppet show, the third graders could demonstrate their understanding of shadows and light sources, for instance, how the puppets' shadows change size and shape when moved closer and farther away from the light. The program gave the pre-K students an introduction to the science of shadows that encouraged curiosity about the subject for them. In this example, students took advantage of the whole school as an inquiry community and fostered learning opportunities between children in different grades as well as peers in their own class. Third graders were surprised at how much the preschool students could understand about light and shadow and had a chance to take the role of expert and teacher for younger students.

In a third example, middle school students worked in small groups to prepare a TV news program based on the ancient Greek myths. They planned to show the program to other 6th and 7th grade classes in the school. During the Create phase of the inquiry, a professional journalist came in as an extended team member from the community to teach students to write different types of news reports. They included a headline story, a sports story, an editorial commentary, a human-interest story, a weather report, and advertisements. Students then rewrote the Greek myths that they had already read and learned about with a contemporary twist. They turned them into new stories for the school TV news program. The news program incorporated script writing and journalistic writing, set design, student drawings, and animations using images of ancient Greek art found from online museum collections.

The Common Core Standards show the increased need for persuasive, explanatory writing genres. These genres are the natural outcome of inquiry learning. When students have deep and rich opportunities for prewriting experiences through the early stages of inquiry, these end products and creations are thoughtful constructions of understanding. Guided Inquiry Design prepares the way for writing and composing to share deep learning with others.

Finding Authentic Audiences

A critical step in creating a product of the inquiry is to identify the audience or audiences that will engage in the sharing. This step must come early in the process of creating a product, perhaps as students identify their inquiry question. Different audiences require different approaches in presentation. Students may create more than one product of their inquiry. They may have a letter or email writing campaign to politicians, a puppet show for younger students in their school or community, a video for peers or a wider Internet audience, and a podcast or oral presentation using PowerPoint for parents all about the same subject. Clearly, although the politicians and parents might enjoy the puppet show, the younger students would not get much out of watching a PowerPoint presentation and could not read or write the letters. Each of these ways of sharing the information allow the learners to articulate important information about what they have learned and provide ways for the learning team to assess the learning.

There may be an audience that is intrinsic to the inquiry topic. If the students have been working on an authentic problem in their community or environment, there may be people who could benefit from the result of the inquiry. In this case, the sharing might take the form of a letter to the editor of the school or local paper, letters and emails to government representatives, or an informative web site about a subject. Students may form a club or extracurricular group as a result of the inquiry. In one instance, a group of 4th grade students who studied issues surrounding water resources started a water conservation club in school, made posters about ways to use water wisely that they posted in the hallways, and met once a month during lunch to continue to share ideas around the topic. The issues that started as "just a school project" became a genuine interest and concern of this group of students for years to come.

Students' classmates in their inquiry community are often a primary audience for sharing their creations. They learn from each other in a well-organized, large-group learning experience that broadens the curriculum content with their important questions and points of view. As they create to share their learning with their peers, students can consider what would be interesting to them and how would they express themselves to this particular social group. Presenters need to consider how they will interest their audience in what they have learned and what will be important for their classmates to know. Students need to keep this audience in mind during the Create phase to make the sharing interesting, engaging, and pertinent. Creating for sharing within school is an important part of the Guided Inquiry process for both the audience receiving the learning and the students who are sharing their learning. Usually individuals and groups are investigating very different aspects under one theme or curricular content. Having an opportunity to hear about the many facets of that topic is useful for the entire inquiry community and has learning value of its own.

The core learning team is another primary audience for creating demonstrations of learning. The learning team will be looking for evidence that the learning goals have been met. Students will need to reflect on the purpose of the inquiry and show how they accomplished that purpose. They need to be guided to demonstrate what they have learned in all five kinds of learning that are accomplished in Guided Inquiry: curriculum content, information literacy, learning how to learn, literacy competency, and social skills. They will need to decide how to show what they have learned.

The extended team members are also a possible audience for the outcome of learning. These people have contributed important aspects to the students' learning in the Guided Inquiry process. They have joined in at critical times with important expertise. The end products help them to see how their piece contributed to the whole. Other audiences within the learning community may be identified as well, such as parents, administrators, and other classes in the school.

School administrators, heads of school, principals, coordinators, and supervisors who have an interest in the success of these students are important audiences to consider including in some sharing sessions. Administrators often can use positive examples of inquiry learning when explaining and promoting the school's Guided Inquiry approach to parents, other administrators, and members of the community. The more they are aware of the deep thought and valuable learning that occurs in Guided Inquiry, the more they are able to be champions and supporters of inquiry learning.

Parents are another audience concerned with the quality of learning of their students. The learning team can set up a way for parents to take a more active role in understanding what their child has learned in Guided Inquiry. This example shows the way one team got parents involved. In the example of students who created a television news broadcast, one audience for the sharing session was students' parents. At the end of that inquiry unit, the learning team invited parents in for a class session to interview their own child's inquiry circle. They provided seven or eight suggested questions, some of which asked about the content and some about the learning process: What was your favorite myth and why? Who was your favorite character in the myths and why? What was the most interesting part of the process? What was the most challenging for you? How did you choose which myths to write about? What do you think you will take away from this experience?

This experience offered students a chance to reflect about the inquiry process to an audience that actually had a stake in what they were saying. Parents heard from the two or three students in their own child's inquiry circle rather than the entire class, which was respectful of their time and interest as well. Parents had a genuine interest in what their child and the circle that he or she worked with closely had to say about what they learned and how they learned it.

Another group of students who conducted an inquiry unit related to global warming and energy efficiency got their parents involved and started a community solar co-op to purchase and install solar panels on houses in the community. Students gain a better understanding of the power of information when they can apply what they have learned to real-life situations and effect change or contribute to a dialogue about issues that are important in their lives, their community, and their world.

Audiences outside the inquiry community may be identified for the inquiry product. Students may want to share their findings with peers in other learning communities. In the information age, the possibilities for this are innumerable. For example, one inquiry community might pair up with an inquiry community in a school in another state or even another country that is learning about the same subject or with a school that has a very different population to provide a different perspective on an issue or topic. Students can Skype or use interactive video conferencing to share their inquiry together. They may want to engage politicians or community action groups in a town meeting or through a video or letter-writing campaign about a problem that was identified in their inquiry that lends itself to social action. The product of their inquiry may be an artwork, performance, or experiment that could be shared with larger audiences in many ways.

What is the Team Doing?

Modeling

The learning team models the pulling together of ideas to find themes, interpret information, and synthesize using many different inquiry charts that match the content and connections (for example, comparison, hierarchy, relations, flow).

Listening

The learning team listens for deep reflections in inquiry circles and connection of thoughts beyond the facts in inquiry journals. They listen for synthesizing ideas and students extending the ideas from their question into their own relevant experiences. They also listen as students begin to tell their story to one another as they share in inquiry circles.

Encouraging

The learning team encourages students to go beyond fact-finding and move into deep reflection on learning through inquiry charts. They encourage each student to create something interesting, unique, and powerful that showcases their learning.

Assessing

The learning team assesses during Create through observation, inquiry journals, conversations in inquiry circles, choices made in the inquiry log, and connections made in inquiry charts to guide students toward synthesizing and communicating their learning.

What is the Learner Doing?

Inquiry Charts: Interpreting

In preparation for Create, students review their inquiry journals to think about what they have learned and decide what they want to emphasize and share in their creations. Inquiry charts are excellent tools for getting ready for Create. They help students to visualize and organize a mixture of many ideas. Inquiry charts help students to organize their thoughts and to visualize connections among their ideas. Graphic organizers, webs, or concept maps are good types of inquiry charts to use for this purpose. Inquiry charts can also help students to decide on a sequence for presenting their learning. Students ask these questions: How do I start? What are my main ideas for the middle? How do I conclude and end? In this case, inquiry charts are similar to informal outlines or flowcharts.

More formal charting in the form of developing patterns to connect ideas such as a web or map is helpful in Create. A variety of shapes and configurations, including comparison, hierarchy, relations, and flow, can be applied depending upon the content and themes. Large circles may represent big ideas, with smaller circles representing subordinate ideas with connecting lines and arrows. Stick figures and various shapes and colors may be used. Inquiry charts can show patterns of similarities as well as anomalies of things that don't fit. Inquiry charts are an opportunity to be inventive, opening up a range of possibilities for students to express their ideas and connections.

Inquiry Logs

Inquiry logs provide citations of the sources students have used and track their choices across the process. Students' inquiry logs are put to use in Create as they quote and paraphrase the sources they have chosen along the way. A list of references of all of the sources used in the inquiry is developed to be included in the presentation. Some of the sources listed in the log may not have been used in the inquiry. Students will need to decide which sources to include in the final list of references.

Inquiry Journals

Students use their inquiry journals to organize and compose their ideas to create a product of inquiry. The journal entries will include drafts of writings, drawings of design concepts, ideas for formats, and questions about what to include in the end product. The journal is used as a place to write partial ideas as they occur and questions there were posed in inquiry circles or to the learning team. The journal is also used to write detailed notes on what students determined to be important from the core sources they chose for deep reading. Now is the time to work through these ideas to compose a story to tell.

Inquiry Community

During Create, the community is buzzing as everyone is working to pull ideas together and create. The tone of the community is of openly conferring. However, most students are working individually on their questions and preparing to share their creations with the entire community.

Inquiry Circles

Create is accomplished in inquiry circles with each small group creating a presentation to share or each individual getting advice from their inquiry circle as he or she creates a presentation. Inquiry circles provide an avenue for constructive critique and peer editing of the product as it is created. Students can use their inquiry circles to try out partially formed ideas or drafts as they develop or to rehearse an oral presentation. The inquiry circles give advice and counsel about whether a presentation is too dry, does not meet the requirements, or needs more information or clarity in a particular area.

Students can take advantage of learning differences in the inquiry circle for creating better presentations. One student may be more gifted at visual understanding, another may be a good descriptive writer, while a third may have an excellent grasp of facts and figures that support an argument. Learners who work in inquiry circles discover that working in collaborative teams helps them to create better end products.

Ideas for Create Sessions

Create sessions are as varied as the types of inquiry and audiences for the inquiry (Figure 9.1). What is essential is that the students are guided to demonstrate what they have learned in a manner that is engaging both to them and to those with whom they are sharing. Many tools are available through technology to assist in the creation and sharing of products with others, and yet low-tech creations can be just as compelling. Students can create video productions, podcasts, blogs, and web pages as well as PowerPoint productions, speeches, or newspaper articles. A product of inquiry could be a community garden, shadow puppet play, or feeding station for migratory birds. A scale model or an artwork may be the most compelling or appropriate creative product of a particular inquiry unit. The product of inquiry could be an exhibition, interactive activity, or game. It may be that students create a low-tech product, such as a scrapbook, newspaper, or dramatic performance, that is then shared with a wider audience through web tools. The school librarian is an invaluable part of the learning team in helping students explore the many and varied tools and ideas for creating products.

Most important, Create in Guided Inquiry is for reflection on learning, interpreting, and extending ideas and for creating in order to communicate ideas. Sessions are designed to accomplish these goals.

What's Next? Sharing

Create is preparation for enlightening Share sessions in Guided Inquiry. Create and Share go hand-in-hand because students need to reflect on their learning and consider their audience before developing a way to share with them. Students use a wide range of media for sharing learning. Share is for the whole inquiry community to learn from each other, broadening the curriculum content to incorporate many important questions, concepts, and points of view.

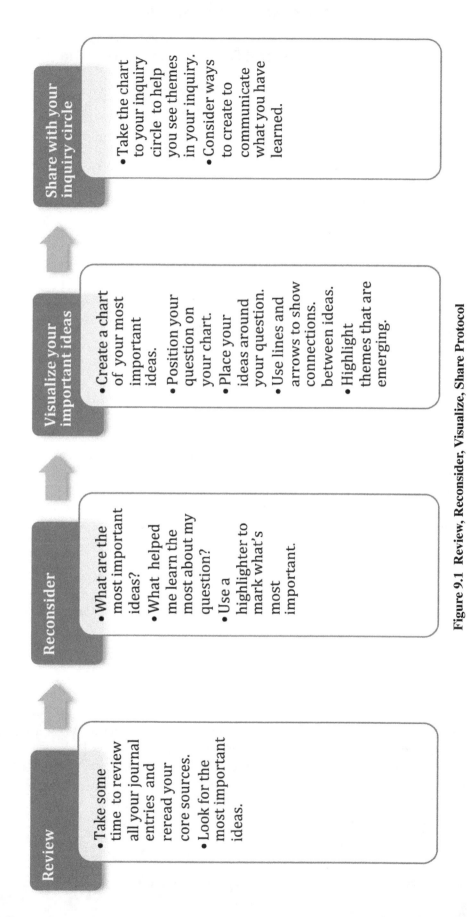

Review

- Take some time to review all your journal entries and reread your core sources.
- Look for the most important ideas.

Reconsider

- What are the most important ideas?
- What helped me learn the most about my question?
- Use a highlighter to mark what's most important.

Visualize your important ideas

- Create a chart of your most important ideas.
- Position your question on your chart.
- Place your ideas around your question.
- Use lines and arrows to show connections between ideas.
- Highlight themes that are emerging.

Share with your inquiry circle

- Take the chart to your inquiry circle to help you see themes in your inquiry.
- Consider ways to create to communicate what you have learned.

Figure 9.1 Review, Reconsider, Visualize, Share Protocol

PAIR SHARE PROTOCOL

Pair Share Protocol Prompts	Go Beyond Facts to Make Meaning
As you reread your core sources and review your journal, think about what you have learned about your inquiry question. Write what these things make you think about your inquiry question.	I learned . . . I think . . .
Read over what you have written and write what you would like to tell someone else about.	I would like to tell about . . .
Pair Share Partner A: Shares. Partner B: Listens and takes notes. Partner B: Shares Partner A: Listens and takes notes.	Share with your partner and take notes. Telling helps you to clarify what you have learned and helps to draw out your own ideas and opinions about your inquiry question.
Partners exchange notes.	Your partner's notes on your telling can give you insight into the meaning of what you have found out and for adding ideas of your own to share what you have learned about your inquiry question.
Reflect on what you learned and how you described it to your partner. Think about creative ways to share your learning with the other students.	Now write what you learned about your inquiry question adding your own thoughts. You also can note some ways to share your learning with others.

Figure 9.2 Create Pair Share Protocol

MODEL SESSION PLAN

OPEN - IMMERSE - EXPLORE - IDENTIFY - GATHER - **CREATE**- SHARE - EVALUATE

Learning Goals: Reflect on learning, go beyond facts to make meaning
Location: School library
Team: Learning team

This Create session applies charting to pull disparate ideas together into a cohesive, meaningful whole. Through charting, the students find themes, patterns, and connections in the ideas and information that they have gathered on their inquiry question

Starter Time: 5 minutes For ideas on charting, refer to *The Back of the Napkin: Solving Problems and Selling Ideas with Pictures* (Roam, 2008)	Before this session students have looked over their inquiry journals, reread their core sources, and reflected on what they have gathered. They have taken time to look at what they have and begun to look for connections. Your students will need several "look" sessions to prepare for the charting session. Introduce the session by explaining that a chart helps us look at what we have to see the connections, patterns, and themes in order to imagine what to Create and to show what to Share. See Roam's steps of visual thinking: Look – See – Imagine – Show. Model charting a concept map from an inquiry question. If you are doing an inquiry in parallel with your class as a model for the process, you can model with one student's work or your own.
Worktime Time: 30 minutes Inquiry chart Inquiry journals You will need poster paper and color markers. Chart may be developed on computer.	Arrange students at tables with large poster paper and color markers. You may want them to sit with their inquiry circle to help get ideas from each other. Students start with their inquiry question as a frame for charting the information from their inquiry journals. Have students take their inquiry journals, especially the notes from the "look" sessions, and chart their most important ideas. Instruct them as follows: Start with your inquiry question and write your question in a box at the center of the poster. Next, place the most important ideas you have learned in boxes on the poster around your question. (They can also use cards so they can move the ideas around.) Think about where you want to place the ideas. Did some ideas give you deeper insight than others? Place these closer to the question and in larger boxes. You don't need to use just words to show ideas. You can also use figures and drawings. What do you begin to see? Do some things fit together? Do some not fit at all? Do some ideas seem most important? Are you seeing ideas intersecting? Overlapping? Connecting? Is one theme surfacing?

Figure 9.3 Create Model Session Plan

	Identify what (connections, interpretations) you see by drawing lines, arrows, circles, colors, and highlights. Be inventive in creating your chart of what you see in understanding your inquiry question.
Reflection Time: 15 minutes Inquiry circle Inquiry chart	Have students bring their inquiry charts to their inquiry circles and share one or two of the most important ideas that surfaced out of the charting. What are the themes, patterns, and connections that surfaced as you charted your ideas and information about your inquiry question? Now consider, so what? Have a discussion with your inquiry circle about: so what? Why is this important to you and what will you Create to tell about it.
Notes:	After this session, have students write in inquiry journal the ideas that surfaced, connections, and patterns or themes that emerged in their inquiry charts and why they are important to them. Arrange conferences with the students for creating to communicate their learning.

Figure 9.3 Create Model Session Plan (*Continued*)

From *Guided Inquiry Design: A Framework for Inquiry in Your School* by Carol C. Kuhlthau, Leslie K. Maniotes, and Ann K. Caspari. Santa Barbara, CA: Libraries Unlimited. Copyright © 2012.

Share

- **Learn from each other**
- **Share learning**
- **Tell your story**

Share

Guided Inquiry Design Process

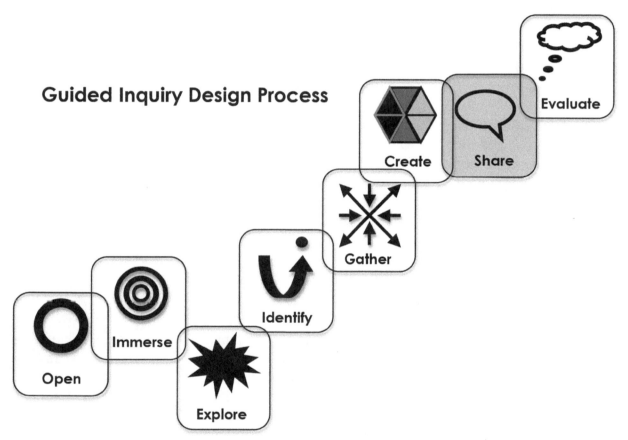

Evaluate

Create   Share

Gather

Identify

Immerse

Open

Explore

Share is the culminating phase in the inquiry process when students share the product they have created to show what they have learned with the other students in their inquiry community. Students have become experts on their question for their inquiry community. They now have the opportunity and responsibility to share their insights with other students and contribute their learning to the whole. Their inquiry products also may be shared with a wider audience, and what they have learned may result in taking an action.

Share is designed so that students share the products they have developed during Create to communicate what they have learned about their inquiry question in an interesting, informative way. An important component of Guided Inquiry is the collaborative learning that takes place when students share what they have learned in the inquiry process. The learning team organizes

Share sessions to provide the best conditions for students to learn substantial content from each other.

The Research

Presentation Stage of the Information Search Process

In the Presentation stage in the Information Search Process (ISP), students completed their search for information and were writing their research paper. They were relieved at having accomplished the research task, but some were anxious about getting their paper written and concerned about getting a good grade. These students viewed the teacher as the sole audience for their papers. One student expressed her disappointment in this. She felt that after all she had learned, she would like to have a wider audience for the things she had found out and the opinions she had formed. She said, "After all I found out, I hate to think of it (my paper) sitting in a drawer. I'd like someone to read it who could do something, like the governor or someone."

When students have learned something important to them, they want to share it more widely with an audience that can have an impact. We can learn something about designing sharing in Guided Inquiry from the ISP. Students' inquiry benefits from a wider audience than just the teacher by taking on importance in their inquiry community and making connections in the world outside of school.

Share in Guided Inquiry

Sharing is a key component of learning in the information age and a capstone of the inquiry process. There are many ways to share information today, and the audiences can come from far and wide. Sometimes the audience is right in the school and other times an audience is across the globe. As schools are changing in the information age, an increasingly important element to sharing in schools is the face-to-face delivery of ideas. This occurs when students share their inquiry and the learning that resulted with the inquiry community. As so much of our lives go online and on the web, it is important that in our community spaces students are taught how to interact in a host of situations. Speaking to a large group or to a small intimate group, creating a short pointed summary of learning through a project, or telling long extended tales of learning processes are all useful life skills. Share sessions are designed to provide opportunities for students to have these kinds of experiences with support and guidance from the learning team so that they can grow their communicative abilities in a wide range of contexts.

Sharing in the inquiry community also happens in all phases across the inquiry process. Sharing with the whole group may be facilitated by web 2.0 tools such as wikis and blogs and are woven in throughout various points in the inquiry. Share and Create are tightly aligned and both are drawn from the Presentation stage of the ISP. They go hand in hand, and what happens in Create informs the Share phase. This chapter provides ideas for guiding sharing, particularly emphasizing face-to-face interactions and demonstrating how Share is designed to work into the learning of the inquiry community and bring the inquiry full circle and to a close.

Learn from Each Other

Sharing is a two-way process that implies more than the delivery of an oral presentation of a research project. When an inquiry community is ready to share what they have been working on, they come together to listen, assess, and contribute to the process so that the learning of each student can continue to deepen and grow. Some say that to teach is to learn, and so the sharing and preparation for sharing deepens the learning for the learners, while at the same time being beneficial for the recipients of the information and giving insights to the community as a whole.

Students can learn substantial content from each other, but much depends on how the Share session is organized and how student learning is presented. The learning team designs Share sessions that enable students to learn. For example, in a biology class in which students were responsible for learning about the different systems of the human body, each inquiry circle chose a particular system to study in depth to share with the rest of the class. Each student identified an inquiry question related to a real-life concern about each of the different body systems. For example, How does this system interact with other systems in the body? How can a person keep this system healthy? What are some of the major diseases or things that can go wrong with this system and why? What recent medical breakthroughs have changed the way we understand or medically treat this system of the body? The learning team knows all the students' projects and designs sessions to pull the ideas together, weaving everything into a coherent whole for the benefit of the entire inquiry community.

In the systems of the body example, students thoughtfully investigated their inquiry questions and shared what they learned about that specific aspect of the system with their inquiry circle by writing a summary and creating a poster. Each inquiry circle then synthesized the key information about their system of the body and provided that information to the whole inquiry community in a creative presentation that included creating a slide show or model or choosing another visual sharing method. Because everyone in the class was responsible for demonstrating understanding about all of the systems of the body, they were attentive and engaged in each other's Share sessions. Students knew the information from one group contributed to the inquiry community's knowledge as a whole.

In the previous biology class example, a technology teacher provided instruction on video production or other presentation technology, the art teacher provided sessions on making models and posters, a museum educator from the science museum led a session on the human body exhibit at the museum, and the reference librarian from the public library helped students locate additional sources. Each of these people became a stakeholder in the inquiry and had something to contribute during sharing.

The main objective of sharing sessions is to learn from each other's inquiry products and celebrate the work that has been accomplished. In a first grade class, students researched and studied different animals, their habitats, and adaptations. Each inquiry circle studied a different habitat and each student chose an animal to research. The class decided to present their information by writing a script and creating videos using Blabberize, in which an image of the animal seems to speak and tell about itself (www.blabberize.com). Each student played his or her video while the rest of the class watched. After each video, students were encouraged to ask questions or make comments about the animal to the student who created the video, with an emphasis on positive comments. This kind of Share session helps to build the inquiry community and gives young students an opportunity to experience the positive support of a learning community and practice in social learning, as well as literacy through listening and responding to other people's work.

The conversations around the sharing are important for highlighting key points, making connections among the ideas in students' presentations, and drawing out central concepts. The core team works together to make the Share sessions rich learning experiences. A successful Share session engages the audience and acknowledges the students' new found expertise as they share what they have learned. Share sessions give everyone in the inquiry community food for thought about ways they might continue to learn about the subject or ways that it could impact their lives. The learning team looks for themes that arise, tying the work together and relating the information as a congruent body of knowledge. Because they are very familiar with the content of all the students' work from the entire inquiry, the learning team sees threads and themes and makes connections for the inquiry community throughout the sessions.

Share the Learning

In many classrooms, teachers organize presentation sessions at the end of a unit as a culminating activity and a way of allowing students an opportunity to demonstrate their knowledge of the subject they have been studying. Share sessions are designed to be authentic and rich learning opportunities for the inquiry community. Share is a time when the inquiry community reflects on the shared learning, analyzes ways to connect the ideas from each of the Share sessions, and builds a conceptual framework for understanding the big ideas of the inquiry unit. The learning team works together with the inquiry community to design engaging sessions that accommodate the needs of that particular group of students within that specific inquiry unit.

There are a number of reasons why the Share sessions are so important to Guided Inquiry. When students learn something interesting, important, and new, it's natural for them to want to share what they know. Guided Inquiry provides a forum for students to learn to effectively communicate their well-reasoned ideas and listen to thoughtful responses from their fellow students in the inquiry community. It is important that they are given the tools to successfully communicate what they've learned. These tools may include presentation techniques, hints for handling stage fright, knowledge of effective formats, and understanding how to communicate to different audiences.

Being able to communicate what one knows is a basic skill for the workplace and community living. Many feel uncomfortable about getting up in front of their fellow students. Some basic presentation techniques are important to learn whatever medium students have chosen to use to communicate. These skills are guided through the considered efforts of the learning team. In one case, the team invited three parents with different kinds of jobs, all requiring performance of one type or another, to form a panel and share memories of times that they had experienced stage fright and techniques they used to persevere and overcome the experience. During the question-and-answer session following the panel, many of the students became more relaxed as they talked through their worries about going on stage. These different types of experts contributed to the feeling of success and readiness for the students leading up to their sharing performance.

Another example of this occurred in a middle school English class where students were exploring Shakespeare's plays and had spent some time understanding *Romeo and Juliet* in various forms. They had decided to perform an adaptation of parts of the ballet for some other classes in the school. The team arranged for members of the local ballet company to work with the students to develop choreography and costumes. Performers and costume designers from the company came to work with the students during several sessions to create the performance.

 Too often, students are asked to create a product without having the advantage of talking to or learning from someone who has done a similar kind of project before. This would not be an optimal approach in the work world.

Share is a time to celebrate. There are many ways to share, from oral presentations to web-based products, Share Fairs, and expositions. In the Guided Inquiry Design Framework, learning is the goal of the Share sessions. When designing Share sessions the team thinks about how to maximize the learning. Inquiry circles can be used, as in the human body example, to share with the whole group or a small group of peers who are interested in the specific content of their presentations or students can pair off for more in-depth learning in a one-on-one session. It's not always necessary for all students to hear every presentation. Sessions are designed to augment learning for each student, with specific goals for the entire inquiry community. When designing the Share phase of the inquiry, the team takes into consideration individual, group, and community needs and interests.

Each Share session includes the opportunity for reflection and audience response. The reflection and response simply might be a question-and-answer period. There might be small-group conversation built in with questions or provocations written by the inquiry circle or developed by the learning team. Online forums often provide opportunities for older students to continue engagement and comments following the sharing session. Audience response is an essential component of Guided Inquiry that keeps the ideas flowing and prevents students from becoming insular. Reflection and response provides opportunities for making connections among presentations to capture the big ideas and important concepts. Through modeling, listening, and encouraging, the learning team guides students' sharing toward analysis and higher-level thinking.

Although essential, student interaction and response requires time management. No one opinion or student should be allowed to take over the session. The learning team along with the inquiry community set boundaries for response. This may mean that each response has a time limit. However, particularly engaging ideas can be noted and revisited at another time or in a different forum. There is no set rule that will apply to all situations. It is the inquiry community that decides the appropriate parameters around sharing under the guidance of the team.

During Share sessions, students may be given a note catcher like the one shown in Figure 10.1. This includes a section for audience members to write what they learned as well as to

STUDENT to STUDENT EVALUATION of SHARE PRESENTATIONS

A listener's response

Name:

Presenter(s): Title of presentation:		Date:
I learned _____.		

Complete the sections below, giving evidence and reasoning to support your opinion.

Effectiveness of presentation	Presentation style	Interest and engagement
Check one • The presentation was effective. I learned something new and it helped me understand the topic. • The presentation was somewhat effective because_____ . • The presentation wasn't very effective because_____.	What I liked about the presentation style was_____. I think they could have____.	What caught my attention was _____. I was interested because _____. I might have been more interested if _____.

Notes:

Figure 10.1 Student to Student Evaluation

evaluate the presentation and offer reasons for their opinions. The notes section includes space for questions or comments that arise during sharing sessions. Having students engage in the sharing in this way continues to engage the community in active learning and assumes participation. As students have learned in their preparation for inquiry circles, notes like these make the conversations that follow much more useful and interesting.

Tell Your Story

Through Guided Inquiry, students are introduced to many different formats that can be useful ways to present knowledge and understanding of a particular subject. Persuasive essays, short punchy oral presentations, and theatrical mixings of powerful images with ideas are all methods of communication that are necessary in the work world and in other forums students encounter in their lives. By this approach, students learn that at times an image, graph, artwork, or interactive experience may be the best way to communicate an idea or point of view. Presentations may take the form of a panel of experts, each with a slightly different point of view or content base. Anyone who has attended a conference has experienced effective presentations as well as disappointingly dismal ones. Students can learn how to engage their audience and discover how enjoyable it can be to share ideas with people who are interested and care about those ideas.

Share is not only a time when students can communicate with each other, Share can also lead to putting newly formed ideas into action. Young people are often overwhelmed by their lack of power in the world and have a great desire to make a difference. This is especially true when they acquire new knowledge and have created an effective way to communicate their ideas about it. They do not want these ideas to be put away and to "sit in a drawer somewhere."

The advantage of working in an inquiry community is the potential to leverage the new understandings and concerns into action. The school has opportunities that individual students would not have. With a certain amount of effort and follow-through, inquiry may lead to action in the community that can have an impact and make a difference. This might mean a community garden in the school that supplements healthier school lunches, a clean water action club that develops awareness of water issues in the community and around the world, or the creation of a community solar co-op that allows community members the chance to incorporate alternative energy sources into the buildings in their community. The Internet offers ways to become connected with causes that have a global impact. Although all inquiry won't lead to "making a garden," through sharing, the inquiry comes full circle back to the students' world and returns to what matters in their lives.

Share is the time to reflect on the "so what" question. What is the importance of these new ideas to my community and me? This question can be answered in ways that are individual, community driven, or global. Not every inquiry needs to answer a global need. The "so what" might be a social project or action or it might be a science experiment that opens up a new concept or it might be evidence of applying a new understanding or skill into the learning process. What is essential is that the learning team looks for evidence that the students have assimilated the knowledge and concepts, can communicate the ideas in informed, thoughtful ways, and use the ideas in new situations or apply them to their own lives.

What is the Team Doing?

The learning team uses modeling, listening, and encouraging to foster third space in the Share phase of inquiry learning. The team models communication strategies, listens to students presentations of ideas, and encourages creativity and risk taking.

Modeling

During Share sessions, the learning team models effective communication techniques by providing all students in the inquiry community with an opportunity to share the products of their inquiry learning and to reflect and respond on each other's findings and ideas. The learning team designs the sessions for success by helping students with time management. Time management and organization are crucial skills for students to learn. The learning team can model short, informative presentations followed by question-and-answer periods or provide samples such as TED talks (www.ted.com), prompted discussions, or other ways to actively engage an audience. In this way, students learn to communicate in organized, thought-provoking, and stimulating ways that are sensitive to the interests of the audience.

The learning team can also manage respectful disagreement when differences of opinion arise within the community. Because the learners become personally engaged with the issues in Guided Inquiry, arguments can erupt over differences of opinion on these issues. The learning team can model the respectful but engaged tone necessary for civil discourse in an intellectual community. In this way, students learn that differences of opinion are a natural part of intellectual engagement and do not necessarily lead to negative feelings about the people who hold a different view. This type of objective discourse is a critical skill in a democratic society and needs to be practiced in the school setting as preparation for life as well as essential for innovating in workplace teams.

Listening

The sharing sessions are a time when an important task of the learning team is listening to students. At this point, the students have completed much of their work and it is time for them to take a lead role, while the learning team listens actively and engages as an audience member. Listening is essential during the reflection and response that follows the sharing session to draw out connections among presentations and to capture the big ideas and important concepts. The learning team listens for opportunities to guide students' sharing toward analysis and higher-level thinking to build a conceptual framework around the inquiry unit.

Encouraging

Most students need encouragement during the sharing sessions due to lack of experience in formally presenting their ideas, stage fright, shyness, or unfamiliarity with a technology tool. The learning team plays a key role at this point in encouraging students and helping them to voice their new knowledge and educated opinions in interesting, creative ways.

Assessing

Although the learning team has many points of assessment during the Guided Inquiry process, Share sessions provide a critical moment for the assessment of learning. The learning team, along with the inquiry community, may use a rubric that they created together to assess whether each student can demonstrate learning of the content, has the ability to organize thoughts and communicate ideas with others in the community, shows an adequate number of quality sources for information, and has an understanding of the importance of the ideas to themselves and the community. Each member of the team will take a greater responsibility for assessment according to his or her own specialty.

What is the Learner Doing?

During Share, students use all the inquiry tools to extend learning in the inquiry community. As students come back together as a group, the community reintegrates the learning from the inquiry and reflects upon the connections among the presentations. Inquiry circles provide constructive feedback in a safe environment of trust that has been built across the inquiry.

Sharing in the Inquiry Community

Share sessions may be organized so either individual students or inquiry circles present the inquiry products to the rest of the inquiry community. The inquiry community forms a supportive environment for students to take risks and hear constructive analysis of their work. As students present their own learning in a creative forum, the other students in their inquiry community respond by building on the ideas.

The students in the inquiry community reflect on the shared ideas, think of ways to connect the ideas from each of the sharing sessions, and begin to build a conceptual framework for the inquiry unit. In this way, the inquiry community is a creative environment for learning and the Share sessions become learning opportunities, not merely the product that is presented for a student to receive a grade.

The inquiry community also plays a role in the assessment of the learning. It is important that students are empowered to critically analyze their own learning and the work of their peers. By assessing each other, students learn to be more reflective, establish a standard of success, and, at the same time, be empathetic toward individuals in the inquiry community. At this time, students will take some notes on assessment so that they will have data or specific ideas and thoughts to present to each other in the evaluation sessions that follow Share.

Inquiry Circles

Share sessions may be arranged so that students share their inquiry products within their inquiry circles. Small group sharing can allow for more active conversations and more indepth reflection. Because the students are more familiar with the work of those in their own inquiry circle, they may be better able to give constructive feedback or assessments of the learning than others in the whole inquiry community. Students may also share from inquiry circle to inquiry circle so that each circle learns from the others. This provides a larger forum than staying within their inquiry circle but keeps the group size smaller than the whole inquiry community.

A combination of sharing in the inquiry community and in inquiry circles can also be effective. For instance, a student may give a five-minute poster or PowerPoint presentation on their inquiry question and then provide discussion questions or conversation prompts for each inquiry circle related to their ideas. At the end of this Share session, students would report back to the inquiry community about the discussions in the inquiry circles. This combination of small and large group activity allows for more diverse perspectives, more in-depth thinking, and more active participation for all students.

Ideas for Share Sessions

There are many different types of Share sessions and products of inquiry (Figure 10.2). The learning team and inquiry community collaborate to consider what type of presentation best fits the audience, the time allowed, and the subject of the inquiry.

Today's technology offers various opportunities for engaging students in a way that a term paper or oral presentation never could. Students can create a video or film documentary or animation using inexpensive equipment. With guidance from the learning team and support from other students in their inquiry community, students can create an engaging multimedia performance with staging, provocative images, and music to convey what they have learned. This type of performance can be shared with other audiences inside and outside the school by videotaping or digital recording. The Internet provides opportunities to create wider audiences that may profit from the product of inquiry through podcasts, blogs, social networking sites, and informative web sites. Interactive video conferencing can provide an opportunity to connect with another inquiry community across the globe.

Although an oral presentation may seem outmoded in this age of technology, face-to-face communication is an essential skill to learn or accomplish. Tools that help students to use both images and words are especially functional. PowerPoint presentations, slide shows, classroom exhibits, or posters can be made in creative, fun, and effective ways. Presentations do not need to be high tech to be worthwhile. A panel discussion, poster session, and small group discussion can provide a useful interaction for a thoughtful exchange of ideas. Students can express their ideas creatively through model-making, artwork, poetry readings, or theater. A variety of creative products can be presented in a coffee house setting that provides a more informal environment for the inquiry community to enjoy and learn from each other's work. Share sessions should take into account the enjoyment that learning brings to students when they are actively engaged, empowered with knowledge, and allowed to express their own ideas in an open and accepting environment.

What's Next? Evaluation

Share sessions in Guided Inquiry are a time of celebration where the learners make contributions to the inquiry community as the inquiry comes to a close. Evaluate follows Share as the inquiry has come to full completion. In Evaluate, students assess their own learning on content and process. They review all the inquiry tools as they reflect on the past cycle of learning. The team also evaluates the learning conferring with students and begins to consider moving the inquiry forward into Build.

MODEL SESSION PLAN

OPEN - IMMERSE - EXPLORE - IDENTIFY - GATHER - CREATE- **SHARE** - EVALUATE

Learning Goals: Share the learning, tell your story, learn from each other
Location: School library
Team: Learning team

This Share session uses a Share Fair for students to learn from each other. A Share Fair is a time to celebrate the learning in the inquiry community at the close of an inquiry unit.

Starter Time: 5 minutes Inquiry community	The learning team welcomes students to the Share Fair. The room is decorated in celebratory fashion related to the theme of the inquiry unit under study. Ground rules for Share Fair are reviewed. The entire inquiry community has created the sharing norms in previous sessions. A purpose for sharing has been established and rules set up so that all have an equal chance to share and get feedback from peers. The team reviews the plan for the session and the norms to follow.
Worktime Time: 40 minutes	Have students break out into groups of five (These can be jigsaw groups, i.e., one from each inquiry circle.). Organize groups so that students are with those outside of the inquiry circle that they have been working with throughout the inquiry unit. Each student in the group has: • 5 minutes to share highlights of their learning • 2 minutes for a question-and-answer session • 1 minute for presenter's final thoughts The group indicates a timekeeper and a secondary timekeeper for when the primary timekeeper is sharing. Each student has 5 notecards on which they write: • Presenter's name • Your name • Two interesting ideas you learned • One question you have These are turned in to the presenter for review and then to the learning team at the end of the session.

Figure 10.2 Share Model Session Plan

Reflection Time: 10 minutes Inquiry journal	Silent reflection and inquiry journal writing time. Have students take a few moments to think about all the ideas that they learned in the Share Fair. Writing prompts: • What important ideas did you learn? • What does it make you think about? • What connections do you make to your own work?
Notes:	Each member of the learning team will not get to hear all of the student presentations. Team members can sit in on one group or rove between groups. The note cards and journal entries will indicate the level to which students engage in the Share Fair.

Figure 10.2 Share Model Session Plan (*Continued*)

Evaluate

- **Evaluate achievement of learning goals**
- **Reflect on content**
- **Reflect on process**

11

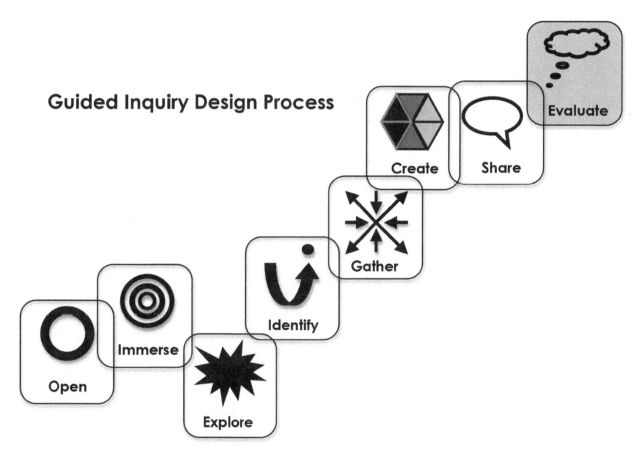

Guided Inquiry Design Process

Open Immerse Explore Identify Gather Create Share Evaluate

The Evaluate phase at the close of the inquiry process is an essential component in Guided Inquiry. Although Guided Inquiry incorporates assessment for determining student progress throughout all stages of the inquiry process, evaluation comes at the end when the learning team evaluates students' achievement of the learning goals.

The learning team also guides students in reflection for self-assessment of their content learning and their progress through the inquiry process. Student self-reflection takes place while the entire process is fresh in their minds to reinforce their content learning and to establish good habits for learning through the inquiry process.

The Research

Assessment of the Information Search Process

In the Information Search Process (ISP) studies, students were asked to reflect on what they had accomplished after the assignment was completed. Most students felt quite satisfied with their progress, but some felt disappointed that their work had not met their expectations. These feelings formed the basis for assessing what went well, what problems were encountered, and how to approach future research assignments. Their reflection on what had taken place during the process and their expectation of what would happen the next time they encountered a similar task made them aware of their own search process.

In later studies, these same students who had come to understand the inquiry process used phrases such as "my process" and the "way I learn." Many also showed an inclination to continue to choose research topics in a similar area in order to build their expertise. For some, this extended expertise even showed evidence of influencing career choices. Guided Inquiry is an efficacious means to achieving today's urgent goal of getting all students college and career ready by having them internalize their inquiry process.

The ISP shows a zone of intervention for evaluating in Guided Inquiry that calls for reflecting on the whole process after everything has been completed. This time of reflection enabled the students to become aware of their own learning process and to see themselves as learning in stages that could be applied in the future.

Evaluate in Guided Inquiry

The end of the inquiry process is the time when the students and the learning team evaluate to determine whether the learning goals have been met. The learning team evaluation is paired with the student self-assessment to give a full account of learning. These two types of evaluation provide both an objective evaluation by the team through the lens of the set criteria for meeting the learning goals and a subjective assessment from the students' perspective of their own learning.

Inquiry tools provide data sources for Evaluate. Inquiry journals give insight into the inquiry process as well as the construction of content learning. Improvement in writing and evidence of learning how to learn are seen in students' inquiry journals. Inquiry logs display the location, evaluation, and use of sources for evaluating progress in information literacy. Inquiry circles provide evidence of student social development in conversation and collaboration. The students' ability to create and share a product of their learning in the inquiry community is an important element of Evaluate at the culmination of Guided Inquiry.

Students' creative products that demonstrate their content learning are important sources for evaluation but are not the only source. The assessment data from inquiry tools used throughout the phases of the inquiry process provide a way of tracking student progress through the process. By the end of the process, the learning team has a fairly good picture of each student's growth and what each student has been able to achieve. The team can also pinpoint where a student has had problems and where more work is needed. Student have accumulated a portfolio of inquiry tools that are evidence of their reflection and construction of content learning as well as the development of their skills, strategies, and abilities in process learning. The Student Learning Inquiry Measure (SLIM) tool kit available on the Center for International Scholarship in School Libraries web site (www.cissl.rutgers.edu/) is a useful tool for collecting data to analyze students learning throughout the inquiry process (for more on SLIM, see Kuhlthau, Maniotes, and Caspari 2007, pp. 126–130). This rich, multilayered picture of student progress provides the body of evidence for evaluating of the whole child. Of course, these holistic process approaches can also be integrated with examinations and tests.

Evaluate Achievement of Learning Goals

The informal assessments and progress monitoring throughout the phases of the inquiry process have provided the learning team with a formative assessment for instructional decision-making *within* the process. It is necessary for the learning team members to have keen observation skills and to systematically collect data across the entire process during conversations and student interactions. The team takes an inquiry stance to teaching as well as to observing and gathering data to be sure to spot where students need assistance and instruction in order to guide the inquiry. The team guides by tailoring instruction conversations and interactions with students directed to these specific needs all along the way.

The accumulation of these data points is an important element of the summative evaluation. The team determines what students have learned in relation to the learning goals decided upon at the outset. There also are aspects of formative assessment in this evaluation that show where students need further improvement. This is the basis for building the Guided Inquiry approach across the curriculum and throughout the grades.

Summative evaluation provides accountability in Guided Inquiry. Questions such as, What did students' learn? Were the learning goals met? are summative questions. Formative questions provide direction for the future. For example, Where do students need to improve? In what areas are they showing weaknesses? How can those areas be strengthened? What were they able to do on their own? What did they need support and more structure to do? These are the kinds of questions that reflective practitioners ask at the end of a unit of study. Taking time to think and reflect in this way is essential for building the next level of student learning in Guided Inquiry that is discussed in more depth in Chapter 12.

Many times the team must focus the evaluation on scores to arrive at grades for each student. To do so, qualitative data must be turned into a number or compared to a rubric for grading. The team can help each other to keep a well-rounded perspective on the integrated learning that happens in inquiry and arrive at grades that appropriately reflect students' work and progress. The team will have determined learning goals for each of the five kinds of learning and set standards for achievement of each goal. When considering learning goals for the five kinds of learning, each element can be parsed out from the integrated whole and a fair grade can be obtained for each area from the holistic learning experience.

The learning team will need to determine what outcomes will indicate that learning goals have been sufficiently achieved. Share sessions provide an opportunity for evaluating demonstrations of learning that students have created and shared. A rubric of criteria, often created

Learning Type	Basic	Approaching	Proficient	Advanced
Content	Repackages information. Reports on unconnected facts.	Mostly reports on facts. Makes some connections between facts.	Shows understanding of content under study. Uses facts and evidence to support ideas, theory, or maintain a position.	Extends concepts and ideas. Demonstrates ability to transfer concepts learned into other areas of study, disciplines, or topics.
Inquiry Process: Learning How to Learn	Shows minimal reflection on own thoughts, feelings, and actions in journal; does not display growth.	Reflects in journals on thoughts, feelings, and actions through the process. Inconsistent use of introduced strategies. Needs support.	Reflects in journal and shows improvement and understanding of own interaction across the process. Applies new strategies to work through process.	Shows growth in understanding of self as learner. Applies strategies and independently chooses strategies to use within the process to learn through inquiry.
Information Literacy	Shows minimal ability to use information literacy skills to impact the learning. Needs further assistance and support.	Inconsistent use of information literacy skills needed in this unit. Some concepts acquired, as evidenced by inquiry tools.	Uses and shows an understanding of information literacy concepts and skills addressed or necessary in this unit.	Applies information literacy concepts and skills addressed to accomplish deeper learning.
Literacy	Employs basic literacy and communication skills throughout the inquiry. Uses some areas of literacy (reading, writing, listening, viewing, and speaking) to participate and learn.	Uses all areas of literacy (reading, writing, listening, viewing, and speaking) to understand material and participate and learn in the inquiry community.	Uses literacy and communication to effectively reflect on inquiry, understand content, collaborate with others, present information, and learn.	Applies literacy and communication skills to show a complex understanding; collaborates with others; creates an impactful argument with support; and shares learning with others. Articulation of reflection shows a growing understanding of self as a learner.
Social	Needs continual support and reminders to contribute and work with others in the inquiry community.	Inconsistently contributes to the inquiry community and inquiry circle. Inconsistent preparation for the meetings. Or needs to work on collaboration.	Contributes as a functioning member of the inquiry circle and inquiry community. Adds to the collaboration.	Actively contributes and participates in all aspects of the inquiry community. Takes initiative for learning and group. Shows empathy and supports others learning.
	1 2	3 4	5 6	7

Figure 11.1 Five Kinds of Learning Rubric

From *Guided Inquiry Design: A Framework for Inquiry in Your School* by Carol C. Kuhlthau, Leslie K. Maniotes, and Ann K. Caspari. Santa Barbara, CA: Libraries Unlimited. Copyright © 2012.

with the students, gives a clear picture of how the work is evaluated. Students need to have a sense of fairness and an understanding of where they have achieved success and where they need to improve as well as how to improve.

In Guided Inquiry, the core team evaluates student progress across all five kinds of learning. The team members apply their specialized expertise to look at the body of evidence throughout the inquiry process. They examine the inquiry tools, the final products, and all work across the inquiry to determine whether learning goals have been met in each of the five kinds of learning: curriculum content, information literacy, learning how to learn, literacy competence, and social skills. Figure 11.1 shows a rubric for the five kinds of learning in inquiry. This rubric can be adjusted and reworked to meet the specific needs of individual inquiries, themes, and more distinct learning goals.

This is a team approach to evaluation that expands upon one teacher's evaluation of an inquiry. The team thinks together about student data to assess individual student learning. There is considerable overlap in the data sources for evaluation of the five kinds of learning that promotes the conversation and consultation among the team members about each student's progress and individual needs. Each team member will be looking at the same set of data but noting different aspects to evaluate students in a particular area of learning. For example, the librarian examines all student work to evaluate progress on information literacy concepts and learning about how to learn through the inquiry process. The subject area teacher looks at the set of data to evaluate the level of understanding of the content knowledge, and a literacy specialist examines the data set to evaluate literacy learning goals.

It is essential that the outcomes match the learning goals and that the learning team is not judging students on an outcome that has not been supported by the learning sessions. When the evaluation is entered with intentionality by the learning team and by the entire inquiry community, it is a natural part of the learning process. This process sets students up for success, gives them the tools they need to achieve, and provides them opportunities to continue to improve from where they are each time they enter the process.

Reflect on Content

Reflection and self-assessment are also natural parts of this phase of the learning process. Many students want to talk about what they learned in their inquiry at this time. An effective way to draw out the essence of the content and their depth of learning about their inquiry question is to start a conversation by asking, what did you find out about your question? From the students' answers to this question, you will be able to tell if students have mainly accumulated disconnected facts or if they have interpreted the facts to come up with a meaningful conclusion. Of course, the age of the child will have some influence, but deep thinking will be easy to spot in students of any age. Taking time to ask the question and gather information on their content knowledge outside the product of inquiry can provide a useful new perspective into what students are taking away from the experience.

Reflecting on each area of learning can have an impact on retention and learning in that area. For example, by reflecting on information seeking and use, students can begin to understand what kinds of sources are useful for finding different types of information, how to evaluate the quality of sources, and how to use information in different content areas. Reflection on learning internally establishes and cements relevant strategies in students' minds. In this case, when brought to attention after the inquiry, strategies for locating, evaluating, and using information at different phases in the inquiry process that underlie information literacy help students to transfer that learning to another context.

Another assessment of the creative product of students' inquiry is their classmates' assessments of what they learned from the sharing. How effective was the student's demonstration of learning for the learning of the inquiry community? Was the presentation style well suited to the information? Did the student present it so that others were interested in the topic and could learn from it? Students' assessment of their process and product in Guided Inquiry gives them an opportunity to reflect on their own work, set goals for themselves, and gain control over their own learning process.

A simple writing prompt asking students to reflect on the content learning can provide the needed information about what students will take away from the inquiry. The prompt can be: What was the central idea of your inquiry? A short paragraph summary statement of the learning will indicate the level to which students go beyond facts to interpreting and drawing connections with their own life.

Reflect on Process

Reflection on the whole inquiry process makes students aware of how they learned through the process (Figures 11.2 and 11.3). This awareness helps them to develop skills and use the tools that are most helpful to them. In the ISP studies, students who were followed up after four years of college referred to "my process" and commented that "this is the way I learn" when asked about how they do research (Kuhlthau 2004). Through reflection at the end of Guided Inquiry, students build an understanding of their own learning process and learning how to learn in the information environment, an essential tool for everyday life as well as for careers and college readiness.

Today, students must learn to be self-directed, motivated inquirers. The overarching goal of Guided Inquiry is for students to become self-directed information seekers with academic skills to succeed in life. This means that they are able to look at multiple sides of a problem and know how to investigate and analyze that problem by using a wide range of quality resources. They make wise choices from a vast information environment to construct new knowledge and articulate and apply their learning in creative, meaningful ways.

To reach this level of sophistication, teachers must involve students of all ages in the task of evaluating their own learning as well as creating goals for continued progress toward the goal of independence. Guided Inquiry helps students become self-reflective and self-directed learners through the gradual release of responsibility for their own learning. When students are aware of their own learning goals and are guided to know what knowledge, skills, and abilities they need to achieve their goals, they are more motivated to work on those skills and much more likely to reach their learning goals.

The studies of students in the ISP show the effectiveness of self-assessment for students' to understand and improve their own research process. Self-assessment is accomplished through reflection on the whole process of inquiry after creating and sharing are completed. Reflection is an essential component of learning in Guided Inquiry. For deep, lasting learning to take hold, learners must pause to reflect on what has been learned before moving on too quickly to

SELF REFLECTION ON INQUIRY

Name:_____

Date:_____

My Inquiry:_____

This is the way I learn
Check the following statements that most reflect how you learned in the past inquiry.

- ○ I need to talk to others about my ideas.
- ○ I need to have some quiet time alone.
- ○ I need some time to think before I write anything down.
- ○ It helps me to draw or chart my ideas.
- ○ I need some help getting going.
- ○ I need to move around.

Give specific examples of the statement(s) here. When did you do this and how did it help you?

My inquiry tools
Complete the sentence

Writing in my inquiry journal helped me to _____ .

My inquiry chart was most useful to me when _____ .

My inquiry log was useful because _____ .

My inquiry circle helped me to _____ .

My inquiry process: This was easy for me:	Because _____ .
This was hard for me:	Because _____ .
Something I will do differently next time is _____ .	Because _____ .

Figure 11.2 Student Self-Reflection on Inquiry

From *Guided Inquiry Design: A Framework for Inquiry in Your School* by Carol C. Kuhlthau, Leslie K. Maniotes, and Ann K. Caspari. Santa Barbara, CA: Libraries Unlimited. Copyright © 2012.

SELF REFLECTION — INQUIRY TOOLS

Name:_____

Date:_____

Teacher:_____

Focus on Inquiry Tools for Learning
Inquiry Tools: Choose the top two tools that helped you the most in this inquiry. Complete the sentence stem to explain how it helped you. Write your reflections in the boxes below. Writing in my inquiry journal helped me to _____ . The inquiry chart was most useful to me when _____ . My inquiry log was useful because _____ . The inquiry circles helped me to _____ . The inquiry community was helpful to me because/when _____ . Inquiry presentations were useful because _____ .
1.
2.

Figure 11.3 Student Self-Reflection on the Use of Inquiry Tools

another project or a different subject. Reflection is built into each inquiry session throughout the inquiry process.

Reflection at the close of an inquiry unit enables self-assessment of the full process, from opening through sharing. When the entire process is still fresh in their minds, students reflect on their progress to consider what caused them difficulty and what they might do differently next time. Timelines are a good way to get students thinking about the stages in inquiry and the different strategies that they used to learn in each of the stages. Knowing how they go through the process, what strategies got them through the difficult parts, and what to look out for in their emotional response to deep learning tasks can help them as they use the inquiry process in all areas of life in and out of school. Becoming aware of their thinking through the process of learning frees them up to recognize their emotional state and choose an appropriate response that will move them forward. Reflecting at the end of the inquiry can help highlight this learning and help them to evolve as a life-long learner.

Reflection on learning at the end of the inquiry is also a way to develop habits of learning how to learn. Students reflect on what they entered into their inquiry journal and how it helped them through the inquiry process or what inquiry chart they used and how it helped them organize information. Using inquiry tools in school is one thing, but providing time to reflect on how the tools helped makes students aware of the purpose and usefulness for them and heightens the likelihood that they might choose to use that tool independently in the future. The goal of Guided Inquiry is to continually grow the learning and understanding of the learning process, each time building on the level of sophistication of the learner and the learning that occurs within inquiry. Prompts, such as What did you think you did well that you would like to replicate in the next inquiry? What would you do differently next time? guide learners to self-monitor their own learning process.

Students can also give valuable evaluative insight into the inquiry for the learning team. It is important for the learning team to gather information from students about what they felt was the most and the least effective aspects of the inquiry. They may have felt rushed at certain points or felt that some aspects of inquiry needed more time. They may have felt the desire for more guidance at certain points. Their perspective may be different from that of the learning team. Students are empowered by knowing that they have a stake in the process and can give feedback that will help the learning team. Asking for their input gives the message that the learning team cares about the students' viewpoints and values their reflections. The students' perspective may be incorporated into changes to improve the way the inquiry is guided for the next inquiry community.

What is the Team Doing?

The team evaluates the learning in this stage. Conferences are set up with each student toward the end of the inquiry from Create to Evaluate as a form of evaluation of learning and to guide students in self-assessment. The team guides the students to analyze all the data sources and, in so doing, evaluates each student's work. The team uses rubrics and conferences as well as the data set of tools to evaluate students' learning about process and content and assigns grades for the work. Sessions are designed to facilitate student self-assessments of learning how to learn and their understanding of content knowledge. Finally, the core team confers together about the various elements of student learning as well as in evaluation of the inquiry as a whole.

What is the Learner Doing?

Students assess their own learning with individual self-reflections on process and content. They review the accumulation of tools in their portfolio to complete a self-assessment of their learning. Students reflect on the use of each tool during inquiry to advance learning how to learn. They use the inquiry journal to document their milestones of learning across the inquiry process as they compose for reflection. Rubrics and self-assessment tools such as timelines and flowcharts help students think about the inquiry in hindsight.

Ideas for Evaluate Sessions

Evaluate sessions may take the form of conversations in the inquiry community (Figure 11.4). The learning team may begin the conversation with prompts that are designed to help the students think back on what they accomplished and on the quality of the process. In this type of session, the whole community reflects together on the common experiences within the process and how the learning goals were met. Care must be taken, however, that a positive tone is continued throughout the inquiry. The learning team is the caretaker for the tone and must make sure that students and instructors continue to be genuinely reflective, constructive, and supportive.

An inquiry circle is an effective tool for assessing the inquiry process. The small groups provide an opportunity for more in-depth conversations and individualized assessments. Each inquiry circle can be provided with a rubric for assessment that encourages reflection, productive conversation, and a critical analysis of the process of learning. The rubric can be created by the learning team or together with the students. They may focus on how the circle worked together and supported the inquiry process.

The inquiry circles are useful for both individual self-reflection and peer critique. By the end of the inquiry, students have developed trust for each other and an understanding of the strengths of each member. They can provide peer guidance that may be more valued by some individuals than teacher criticism. During the inquiry circles, the learning team rotates through the circles to listen in and gather data on conversations that are reflective and constructive and provide guidance when needed.

The learning team conducts individual conferences for Evaluate. For some students, it may be important to have quiet time to reflect on personal gains and struggles and to take that learning into the next inquiry. Inquiry learning is a personal learning process even though it occurs in a social context. Conferences with students, paired with a self-assessment, are an ideal way to capture the individual experience of learning. Prior to conferencing, students complete an individual inquiry assessment. This can be a survey, checklist, or brief written analysis based on the rubric to prepare for the conversation. Conferencing has the advantage of providing a private forum to students who are less comfortable critically analyzing their own learning in a larger group. Conferences can be effectively arranged with each student through scheduling from the Create phase through Evaluate.

What's Next? Building Guided Inquiry

In Guided Inquiry one inquiry leads to another building strategies, knowledge and skills in a continuum through the grades. Where students need improvement becomes evident in Evaluate and the basis for building the next level of student learning. The next chapter, Build, explores the possibilities in Guided Inquiry beyond one inquiry project into a school-wide systematic approach to learning.

MODEL SESSION PLAN

OPEN - IMMERSE - EXPLORE - IDENTIFY - GATHER - CREATE- SHARE - **EVALUATE**

Learning Goals: Reflect on process
Location: School library
Team: Learning team

In this Evaluate session, students are guided through reflection on the entire inquiry process with the goal of developing competency in learning how to learn.

Starter Time: 5 minutes	Before this session, students have looked over their inquiry journals to recall what they were doing, thinking, and feeling at the beginning, middle, and close of their inquiry process. They highlighted these with color markers or sticky notes. Introduce the idea that when they reflect on their learning experiences, they develop as self-reflective learners. Encourage them to recall and reflect on what went well and why as well as when they had difficulty and why. Ask students to think of what they found in their inquiry journals as a timeline of their experience that they can share in their inquiry circle. Prompts for inquiry circle conversation: At the beginning, middle, and the end of your inquiry process: • Thoughts: What were you thinking about? • Actions: What actions did you take? • Feelings: How did you feel?
Worktime Time: 20 minutes Inquiry circle	Have students join their inquiry circles to share what they found in their inquiry journals about their thoughts, actions, and feelings at the beginning, middle, and end of the inquiry unit. Ask them to share examples from their journals that describe changes they noticed at these times in their learning process. Encourage them to share difficulties along with successes. Ask each inquiry circle to prepare to share their examples with the whole group by organizing their experiences to describe what happened around the three points of their inquiry.
Reflection Time: 20 minutes Inquiry community	At the top of three large posters write Beginning of Inquiry, Middle of Inquiry, Close of Inquiry and write Thoughts, Actions, Feelings as headings for students' comments under each. As the students in each inquiry circle share their examples, build a timeline on the posters of students' reflections and examples. After all of the circles have shared their thoughts, actions, and feelings at the three points in the inquiry process, review the timeline with the students. Explain that they have created a timeline of their self reflections on the inquiry process that they went through.

Figure 11.4 Evaluate Model Session Plan

	Have students think about and respond to these questions: • What have you learned about the inquiry process? • What did you do well that you would repeat in the next inquiry? • What will you do differently next time?
Notes:	In another session, have students write a reflection on what content they learned. Ask students to write a short paragraph about the central idea of their inquiry. A short summary statement of the learning will indicate the level that students have gone beyond facts to interpret and draw connections with their own lives. This is a good supplement to the products of inquiry that students have created to evaluate their content learning.

Figure 11.4 Evaluate Model Session Plan (*Continued*)

Building Guided Inquiry in Your School

12

Guided Inquiry is extended beyond one inquiry unit and built into a way of learning across the curriculum and throughout grade levels. Evaluation at the close of the Guided Inquiry process reveals what students have mastered and where they need more guidance, instruction, and practice. In this way, each inquiry learning experience builds on the one before. Guided Inquiry teams work to connect and integrate curricular goals and develop a scope and sequence for learning across a year and across grade levels. The ideal is to scaffold learning from early grades through secondary school, with sufficient flexibility to meet individual student's needs and abilities through an inquiry approach.

The Guided Inquiry process ends by opening to more topics, ideas, and questions for further inquiry. These questions lead to constructing understandings and deepening learning rather than arriving at final solutions or finite answers. Meaningful inquiry questions introduce new topics for immersing, more interesting ideas for exploring, and identification of other important questions for gathering, creating, and sharing. The close of one Guided Inquiry process opens a range of possible new ones. In this way, the Guided Inquiry is cyclical and ongoing.

Traditional approaches rarely open new questions at the end of a unit of study. Typically students and teachers move to an entirely new topic once a project is "complete." The Guided Inquiry Design Framework provides a way to arrange the curriculum so that one inquiry leads into the next, building the learning outward in a natural progression of connection and continuity for deeper understanding and learning.

Evaluation is formative as well as summative, revealing what students learned and what they need to learn. Guided Inquiry provides a framework for building a scaffold through the grades in all five kinds of learning thus applying inquiry tools as strategies for relevant engaged deep learning in the information age.

The Research: Follow-up Studies of the Information Search Process

Findings for College and Career Readiness

Extending inquiry units into an approach that expands throughout the grades, as described above, prepares students for college and career readiness. The research in studies of post-secondary students shows the value for students when they engage in meaningful inquiry during school years. The high school students in the original information-seeking study were studied four years later to investigate how they had fared in their research assignments in their undergraduate college years and their perceptions of the Information Search Process (ISP) (Kuhlthau 2004, p. 71). The findings from this study have implications about Guided Inquiry across the grade levels. These longitudinal studies found that students:

- Preferred to choose their own topics rather than being given a topic "out of a hat" or "by a lottery."

- Built research topics on prior research papers. Although this may have been an attempt to make the task easier, it also indicated an area of specialization and movement toward developing expertise in certain subjects. Where possible, they chose topics related to the careers for which they were preparing.

- Wanted to share what they had learned beyond school and relate it to the real world. They did not want to just drop it and move on but rather to do something more with what they had learned.

- Had internalized the research process as their own. "This is my process and this is the way I learn." They had an understanding that the process of learning from a variety of sources of information was not just finding and reproducing texts.

- Saw this as a way of learning in the information age that they took into the work place. They had internalized concepts that transferred to other situations of information use.

Further longitudinal studies tracked students into their jobs in the workplace. These studies found that an understanding of the stages of the ISP was helpful in more complex information-intensive work tasks. Participants saw the benefit of internalizing the stages of the ISP in these information tasks that called for putting ideas together in an innovative and creative way that added value to a project rather than just reporting on facts (Kuhlthau 2004, p. 165).

These studies show the long-term advantages of building Guided Inquiry beyond one inquiry process into a way of learning in the information-age school. Students wanted to be involved in choosing their research topics and had used their research assignments to grow expertise and learn how to learn. As a result of their inquiry experience in school, they were able to transfer the learning to their academic and career lives. These studies show the powerful outcome of building the Guided Inquiry process as a way of learning in your school to prepare students for academic achievement and career readiness.

Building Guided Inquiry: Content and Process

There are two components to building Guided Inquiry. The first is related to the content of the inquiry where connections are built between inquiry units of study. Guided Inquiry doesn't end with one inquiry unit. The content builds from one inquiry to the next, at times extending into a related area of the subject such as another theme or time period, other times leading into another subject in the curriculum. These connected, extended inquiries provide students with broad integrated knowledge as well as opportunities for developing their own areas of personal specialization and expertise. Students in the ISP studies preferred to choose their own topics, build on what they had done before, and share what they had learned. When students take inquiry seriously, they see it as an opportunity to study what is personally interesting and relevant to them and connected to their outside-of-school experiences and lives in the third space. A program of Guided Inquiry is built on these ways of organizing the content of learning to engage students in their own stream of inquiry for deep and lasting understandings.

Building inquiry can happen within a subject, as when younger students who are learning about shadows and light begin to wonder about the sun, the moon, and why we see phases of the moon. The learning team notes that the students have developed new inquiry questions that can be further explored. This might also lead to an interdisciplinary exploration. The inquiry that started as a science inquiry could become a science and literature examination of poetry related to shadows or the moon. For high school students, a Guided Inquiry that was built around the book *Fever 1793* by Laurie Halse Anderson might start with the learning team of the school librarian along with an English teacher and a social studies teacher exploring character development and early American history. This inquiry could lead to a study of epidemics that involved collaboration between the school librarian, social studies teacher, and biology teacher and spanned across American or world history. In each case, the learning team must be alert to the possibilities of connections and the developing interests of the students as they emerge through the inquiry process.

The second component to building Guided Inquiry concentrates on the process of learning from a variety of sources of information. The emphasis here is on the Guided Inquiry process. A goal of Guided Inquiry is to enable students to gradually internalize the learning process as their own. Students learn that using information is not just finding and reproducing texts but involves reflecting, interpreting, thinking, and creating. By consistently learning through the phases of the Guided Inquiry process, students gain competence and independence for taking responsibility for their own learning process. Internalizing the Guided Inquiry process as a way of learning gives students an extraordinary advantage for success in advanced academic challenges and in the changing workplace of today's information environment.

Culmination Conversations for Building Guided Inquiry

Culmination conversations about learning at an end of the inquiry unit serve a variety of purposes. The learning team comes together to talk about the data they have collected from students throughout the inquiry process. In the Evaluate phase of the Guided Inquiry process, the purpose is to examine how well students were able to accomplish the learning goals of the inquiry and to communicate to each student how well they achieved the goals. Culmination conversations also have the more far-reaching purpose of designing for growth across the curriculum and across the grade levels of the school to make a long-term difference in learning for students. These conversations are critical elements for reflective practitioners in developing the scope and sequence for Guided Inquiry that meets the learning needs of students as they move from grade to grade.

The culmination conversations center first on what went well and what worked and resulted in achieving the learning goals. Next, the team needs to identify any difficulties that students experienced with any one aspect of the inquiry. It is important to discuss problems that students had in any one area so that the succeeding inquiry continues to improve upon and grow students' skills and knowledge. For example, if there were major misconceptions about content or process at the outset, the team will want to consider whether these misconceptions were rectified in the inquiry process and how these were clarified.

The learning team will need to consider students who did not make sufficient progress in their understanding of the inquiry process, did not dig deeply enough into content, or were unable to be articulate about their learning. The team discusses ways to solve these students' problems to ensure all students are learning and growing to their fullest capacity. When the evaluation of Guided Inquiry homes in on the progress of individual students, the team considers next steps for improving learning. The outcome of this meeting is to come up with an action plan for the learning that is flowing into the next inquiry unit. The action plan addresses the design of instructional strategies and the learning environment to better meet the needs of all students. The information developed at this time may be useful in determining the makeup of the inquiry circles for the next inquiry unit or the level of guidance around specific skills.

Culmination conversations look broadly at the whole group of students in all five kinds of learning: curriculum content, information literacy, learning how to learn, literacy competency, and social skills. Once each member of the learning team has carefully gone over the data from the students' inquiry tools, they bring their analysis, assessments, and evaluations to the table, each from the perspective of their specialization. For example, in the three-member team comprised of the social studies teacher, literacy teacher, and the school librarian, the literacy teacher examines the data, considering improvement in reading, writing, and other literacy competencies. The social studies teacher looks at how the inquiry deepened understanding of specific areas of the unit content, and the school librarian gathers evidence on information literacy skills and how the students learned through the phases of the inquiry process. They all convene at the end of the inquiry for a culmination conversation. This conversation includes overall trends about the learning across all areas in order to consider how the learning was structured and guided as well as what improvements might be made for the next inquiry unit. This whole team's reflection on the learning is used to ensure that Guided Inquiry is continually meeting the needs of all students in all five kinds of learning.

One way to organize the culmination conversation is like a round robin sharing session. In this case, more specific areas of learning may be targeted for analysis. For example, the literacy teacher kept an eye on specific students who were having trouble with literacy concepts throughout and brings that data to the culmination conversation. The social studies teacher was looking at the whole group of students and getting a general feel for how the group was learning concepts and applying facts. And the school librarian was focusing on a specific concept within information literacy. Though each member of the team is gathering different data on these students, the learning conversation incorporates the three team members' perspectives on the students and particular aspects of their learning through the inquiry unit. Each member of the team takes ten minutes to share the learning from his or her own perspective. At the end, trends and themes are discussed to decide how to build Guided Inquiry to improve learning in these specific areas.

In addition, the learning team analyzes the data collected from students to reflect on the teaching/facilitation process. The team evaluates the effectiveness of the Guided Inquiry approach to identify ways to refine and improve guidance for future inquiry projects. In this way, the team is continually planning ways to improve learning and advance the Guided Inquiry to better meet the learning needs of each student. The culmination conversation evaluates the structure of the inquiry unit (Figures 12.1 and 12.2). This is more of a reflective evaluation of instruction, guidance, and intervention. In this conversation, the team analyzes the data to see what instructional moves made a difference for this group. The team might consider a problem such as how these students used questions across the process or how students transferred what

Culmination Conversation
Agenda

Team Members:		Date:
Inquiry Unit:		
Time Keeper:		

Item	Topic	Time
Whip Around . . . of general impressions from rubric	Each team member has 3 minutes to reflect on overall learning.	10 minutes
Group Reflection	Each team member takes time to discuss data on learning in the inquiry unit.	30 minutes
Action Plans	The team agrees upon one actionable item for each team member.	5 minutes
Closing Thoughts	Summary of discussion. Or one actionable item for the next inquiry is agreed upon. Actionable item for learning or working as a collaborative team. We agree that next time we will _____ .	5 minutes

Figure 12.1 Culmination Conversation Agenda

From *Guided Inquiry Design: A Framework for Inquiry in Your School* by Carol C. Kuhlthau, Leslie K. Maniotes, and Ann K. Caspari. Santa Barbara, CA: Libraries Unlimited. Copyright © 2012.

Culmination Conversation Agenda
(with Target Group)

Team Members:		Date:
Inquiry Unit:		
Time Keeper:		

Item	Topic	Time
Whip Around ...of general impressions from rubric	Each team member has 3 minutes to reflect on the overall learning.	10 minutes
Target Group Discussion: **Target Students:**	Each team member takes time to discuss data on each of these students in turn.	30 minutes
Action Plans	The team agrees upon one actionable item for each student. Team decides upon which member will confer with the student to discuss the learning goals going forward. Student name　　　　Action　　　　Team member	5 minutes
	1.		
	2.		
	3.		
	4.		
	5.		
	6.		
Closing Thoughts	Summary of discussion. Or one actionable item for the next inquiry is agreed upon. Actionable item for learning or working as a collaborative team. We agree that next time we will _____ .	5 minutes

Figure 12.2 Culmination Conversation Agenda with Target Group

the learning team modeled into their own work. This culmination conversation helps the team to become more effective teachers within the Guided Inquiry process and builds a learning community outward to the school level as instructional practice is examined related to student learning across each inquiry unit.

Organization of the culmination conversations is essential to accomplishing these goals. It is necessary to have clear meeting objectives prior to the scheduled date so team members come prepared and the conversation remains focused and productive. Taking time to prepare for culmination conversations is extremely important for making effective use of in-meeting time. Protocols are useful to help the team stay on point. The National School Reform Faculty has a wide variety of protocols that are helpful for talking about learning, using data, and working together collaboratively to improve learning (http://www.nsrfharmony.org/protocols.html).

The key to a productive conversation is that it focuses on data and that a goal for the conversation is established so the learning team comes away from the conversation with a new perspective on the past inquiry learning that they can apply to the next inquiry unit. It is also important to allow the data to show what needs improvement and that the team continues to work together to improve teaching and learning through Guided Inquiry. Arriving at agreements at the close of the meeting will keep the team on track for moving forward and growing together to meet the learning needs of all students. Agreements should be actionable steps that each member can take to improve the facilitation of learning through Guided Inquiry.

As the culmination conversation progresses, it is important to capture the ideas that are being discussed. During the conversation, the team will need to take notes, make lists, and chart what worked and what needs improvement in the inquiry unit. These notations provide valuable information for designing the successive Guided Inquiry units for these students and for the next group of students to learn in this inquiry unit. In addition, it is important to accumulate the notes from multiple culmination conversations following each inquiry unit with different groups of students in a variety of subjects. These notations, lists, and charts provide the documentation for building a Guided Inquiry approach in your school. Over time, the documentation from the culmination conversations can be developed into a Guided Inquiry scope and sequence across the curriculum and across the grades tailored for the students in your school.

Building Guided Inquiry as a Way of Learning Across the Grades

The design of Guided Inquiry should become increasingly more sophisticated across the grades. Each inquiry unit is designed to ensure more meaningful integration of content and process building on the previous learning. This is not a new concept but it does need particular attention and consideration in all five kinds of learning in Guided Inquiry.

The Common Core State Standards recognize the need to integrate learning in all areas of the curriculum. *The Common Core State Standards for English Language Arts & Literacy in History/Social Studies, Science, and Technical Subjects* indicates the urgency and necessity of this integrated view of learning in schools. The standards are a good example of how to build knowledge over time and across grade levels by designing learning experiences that build core knowledge from one grade to the next. The section "Staying on Topic Within a Grade and Across Grades: How to Build Knowledge Systematically in English Language Arts K-5" (p. 33) explains it this way:

Building knowledge systematically in English language arts is like giving children various pieces of a puzzle in each grade that, over time, will form one big picture. At a curricular or instructional level, texts—within and across grade levels—need to be selected around topics or themes that systematically develop the knowledge base of students. Within a grade level, there should be an adequate number of titles on a single topic that allow children to study that topic for a sustained period. The knowledge children have learned about particular topics in early grade levels should then be expanded and developed in subsequent grade levels to ensure an increasingly deeper understanding of these topics. Children in the upper elementary grades will generally be expected to read these texts independently and reflect on them in writing. However, children in the early grades (particularly K–2) should participate in rich, structured conversations with an adult in response to the written texts that are read aloud, orally comparing and contrasting as well as analyzing and synthesizing, in the manner called for by the *Standards*.

Guided Inquiry should be conceived and designed to build knowledge of content and process in this scaffold way. The knowledge children learn through Guided Inquiry of specific questions in early grade levels is expanded and developed in subsequent grade levels to ensure an increasingly deeper understanding of these questions as well as a deepening understanding of their own process of learning from a variety of sources of information. The many concepts underlying information searching, evaluation, and use, as well as the process of learning, cannot be gained in one inquiry project per grade level. The students need consistently well-designed coherent Guided Inquiry sequences that build on prior learning. Over time, deep learning of curriculum content incorporates fact-finding with interpreting and synthesizing in discipline-specific areas. Students' information literacy gradually develops through their consistent experience with underlying concepts for locating, evaluating, and using information wisely. Their personal sense of learning how to learn is gradually internalized through repeated experiences in the inquiry process across the grades. Their competency in reading, writing, speaking, listening, viewing, and presenting gradually develops through many years of practice in the Guided Inquiry process. Continued situations that require interacting, cooperating, and collaborating in successful sustained group work and within a wide variety of contexts develops social skills. Each of these kinds of learning will need to be thoughtfully structured in Guided Inquiry across the grades to give students all of the "pieces of the puzzle to form the big picture" for learning, working, and living in complex information environments.

Building the level of understanding from pre-K through secondary school is the vision of Guided Inquiry for all students in the information-age school. The American Association of School Librarians Learning *Standards for the 21st Century Learner* (2007), as well as Partnership for 21st Century Skills, share this vision of learning in schools today. The standards show what students need to learn, while the Guided Inquiry Design Framework shows teachers how to structure learning in schools to accomplish this vision.

Building a Collaborative School Culture

In order to accomplish this vision of learning through Guided Inquiry, a collaborative culture must be simultaneously built in schools. Today many tech-savvy teachers are reaching out to one another on Twitter and sharing resources in professional learning networks that span the globe. However, too often local in-school structures continue to isolate teachers in an old paradigm. Guided Inquiry schools require the collaborative teaching and learning environment of an inquiry community. The schools must create structures that support flexible learning teams that have time to design, implement, and reflect together. There needs to be a commitment at the school level to include the extended team of experts in learning. The extended team works alongside the core team to expand the expertise and resources for learning. Schools must have their core values centered on learning in the third space. This means that students' academic learning is consistently linked to their interactions in the world. Educators must have a complex understanding of how the community outside the school can enhance curricular and academic learning and value and intentionally access these real-world connections.

Priorities need to change from compliant behaviors to an innovative professional culture where the top priority is learning that helps students engage in the world today. The priority in inquiry schools depends on collaboration, flexible organization, and information literacy. Teachers must be dedicated to and purposeful in maintaining an inquiry stance in teaching and learning. Through a school-wide collaborative culture, educators can help one another to use the strategies that encourage third space and develop the inquiry mindset explained here. Teachers need to be creative in modeling, listening, encouraging, and questioning students to build the inquiry approach. School librarians need to provide leadership in transforming schools into information-age learning communities by taking on the essential role of information learning specialist. As the collaborative culture grows in the school, teachers and school librarians can establish norms that will help them to support each other in building Guided Inquiry into a sustainable school-wide approach.

Getting Started and Sustaining Change

In *Guided Inquiry: Learning in the 21st Century,* we concluded the book offering three recommendations for establishing Guided Inquiry that are worth repeating here:

- Gain systemic support
- Develop an implementation plan
- Create a Guided Inquiry network

The first is to gain systemic support. For Guided Inquiry to take hold, it must be embraced by the entire school community and include all stakeholders. In many schools, it is the principal, head of school, and other administrators who bring Guided Inquiry into the school. In other schools, it is the school librarian or teachers who first introduce Guided Inquiry. Whoever initiates Guided Inquiry, it will depend on the full support of the administration, teachers, and school librarians for success in one inquiry to be built into a whole-school Guided Inquiry approach.

The second recommendation is to develop an implementation plan that lays out how you will make the change to Guided Inquiry in your school. Begin with where you are now and where you would like to be in three years and the steps you will take to get there. The Guided Inquiry Design Framework is an essential tool for building Guided Inquiry for the students in your school. Continual professional development and training will be a necessary component in your implementation plan. Building a Guided Inquiry scope and sequence that matches your curriculum is an important part of that implementation plan.

The third recommendation is to create a Guided Inquiry network in your school for sharing the culmination conversations from each inquiry unit. This in-school network is essential for building Guided Inquiry across the curriculum and across grade levels tailored to the students in your school. This networked approach can be extended from the school to the district and beyond in collaboration and support of the approach, expanding resources, and sharing findings from research on practice.

Building Guided Inquiry in Your School

We are at a critical crossroads in education. All sectors of society are turning to education to solve a multitude of pressing problems. Educating students for the future has always been important but it is a particularly high calling at this time. For our children and teens to grow into productive citizens with successful lives, they need to have expertise in multiple literacies and a wide range of competencies for a changing, uncertain world. They need to be able to think, learn, and create and be able to search, evaluate, and use information for doing so. They need schools that give them opportunities to do this daily in every subject of the curriculum. They need to see the connection with what they are learning in school with the world outside of school that motivates them to stay in school and do their best. Inquiry has become the buzzword in schools to meet this challenge. But teachers are asking, how do we do it?

Guided Inquiry is an exciting new form of teaching and learning that has emerged at this critical time for education. Our book *Guided Inquiry: Learning in the 21st Century* explained what Guided Inquiry is and why it is essential now. This book gives you the framework for designing Guided Inquiry for the students in your school. But the work is not done. Guided Inquiry is out of our hands and in the hands of learning teams and creative educators around the world who want to make a change for the better. Now the real work begins in your school, with your team taking the framework to design inquiry for each phase in the inquiry process specifically tailored to your students' learning needs. Guided Inquiry prepares a future generation for an uncertain, changing world by giving them the education for thinking and learning through multiple sources of information for seeking meaning in that changing, uncertain world.

List of Resources

(by chapter in order of appearance)

Chapter 3, Inquiry Tools

Visual Understanding in Education, Visual Thinking Strategies (http://www.vtshome.org/)
Reading Quest (http://www.readingquest.org/strat/)
Thinking maps (http://www.thinkingmaps.com/)
Education Place (http://www.eduplace.com/graphicorganizer/)
Scholastic (http://www2.scholastic.com/browse/article.jsp?id=2983)
www.nationalgeographic.com

Chapter 4, Open

Johnson, L. 2010. The Burden of Thirst. *National Geographic Magazine*, April
(http://ngm.nationalgeographic.com/2010/04/table-of-contents)
(http://ngm.nationalgeographic.com/2010/04/water-slaves/johnson-photography)
(Accessed July 18, 2011)
Smithsonian American Art Museum, "Boys in a Dory, Winslow Homer."
(http://americanart.si.edu/collections/search/artwork/?id=73938) (Accessed July 18, 2011)
Library of Congress American Memory (www.loc.gov)
Ted Talks (www.ted.com)
Radiolab (www.radiolab.org)

Chapter 5, Immerse

PBSKids, Sid the Science Kid, Shadow Investigation (http://pbskids.org/sid/videoplayer.html)
The Grapes of Wrath (Steinbeck, 1939).
Bud not Buddy (Curtis, 1999)
National Building Museum, Bridge Basics
(http://www.nbm.org/assets/pdfs/youth-education/bridges_erpacket.pdf)

Chapter 6, Explore

National Zoo, Smithsonian Migratory Bird Center, Bridging the Americas
(http://nationalzoo.si.edu/scbi/migratorybirds/education/teacher_resources/bridging_the_
americas/default.cfm)
Jog the Web (Jogtheweb.com)
Livebinder (Livebinder.com)

Chapter 7, Identify

Wordle.net

Chapter 9, Create

Microsoft Word, Smart Art Graphics Gallery

Chapter 10, Share

Blabberize (http://blabberize.com)

References

American Association of School Librarians. 2007. *Standards for the 21st Century Learner*. Chicago: American Library Association.

Bhabha, H.K. 1994. *The Location of Culture*. New York: Routledge.

Common Core Standards Initiative. Available at http://www.corestandards.org/. Accessed July 29, 2011.

Gallas, K. 1995. *Talking Their Way Into Science: Hearing Children's Questions and Theories, Responding with Curricula*. New York: Teachers College Press.

Kuhlthau, C.C., Maniotes L., and Caspari, A. 2007. *Guided Inquiry: Learning in the 21st Century*. Westport, CT: Libraries Unlimited.

Kuhlthau, C.C. 2004. *Seeking Meaning: A Process Approach to Library and Information Services*. 2nd ed. Westport, CT: Libraries Unlimited.

Kuhlthau, C.C.1985. *Teaching the Library Research Process*. New York: The Center for Applied Research in Education, 2nd ed. Scarecrow Press, 1994.

Maniotes, L.K. 2005. *The Transformative Power of Literary Third Space*. Doctoral dissertation, School of Education, University of Colorado, Boulder.

Maybin, J. 1999. Framing and Evaluation in Ten- to Twelve-Year-Old School Children's Use of Repeated, Appropriated, and Reported Speech in Relation to Their Induction into Educational Procedures and Practices. Text, 19, 4, 459–484.

Roam, D. 2008. *The Back of the Napkin: Solving Problems and Selling Ideas with Pictures*. New York: Penguin Books.

Todd, R., Gordon, C., and Lu, Y. 2010. *NJASL Research Study, One Common Goal: Student Learning*. Report of Findings and Recommendations of The New Jersey School Library Survey.

Todd, R., Kuhlthau, C.C., and Heinstrom, J. 2005. *Impact of School Libraries on Student Learning*. Institute of Museum and Library Services Leadership Grant Project Report http://cissl.scils.rutgers.edu/research/imls.

Wells, G. 2000. Dialogic inquiry in education: Building on the legacy of Vygotsky, pp. 51–85. In C. D. Lee and P. Smagorinsky, eds. *Vygotskian Perspectives on Literacy Research: Constructing Meaning Through Collaborative Inquiry*. Cambridge, UK: Cambridge University Press.

Index

Numbers in *italic* type indicate a figure or table.

About the Authors

Carol C. Kuhlthau is professor emerita of Library and Information Science at Rutgers University, where she directed the graduate program in school librarianship, rated number one in the country by *U.S. News & World Report*. She is founding director of the Center for International Scholarship in School Libraries at Rutgers University, where she serves as senior advisor. Her published works include Libraries Unlimited's *Seeking Meaning: A Process Approach to Library and Information Services,* second edition, and *Guided Inquiry: Learning in the 21st Century*. Kuhlthau is internationally recognized for her groundbreaking research on the Information Search Process and the ISP model of thoughts, feelings, and actions in six stages of information seeking and use.

Leslie K. Maniotes, PhD, is an educational leader in the Denver Public Schools. A National Board Certified Teacher with 11 years of classroom experience, Maniotes has also worked as a Teacher Effectiveness Coach and a K–12 literacy specialist in rural and urban Title I schools. She received her doctorate in curriculum and instruction in the content areas from the University of Colorado, Boulder, and master's degree in reading from the University of North Carolina, Greensboro. She is a nationally known educational consultant on the Guided Inquiry approach, leading teams to improve learning and inquiry design by integrating workshops and coaching. Her published works include Libraries Unlimited's *Guided Inquiry: Learning in the 21st Century* and various articles on inquiry learning and literacy learning. @lesliemaniotes on twitter and http://web.me.com/lesliekm/Site/Welcome.html.

Ann K. Caspari is education specialist at the Smithsonian Institution's National Air and Space Museum and director of a professional development program for preschool teachers in the District of Columbia Public Schools on inquiry science for young learners. With more than 20 years of experience in museum education, Caspari has worked in diverse institutions such as the National Building Museum in Washington, D.C., Calvert Marine Museum in Maryland, and the Paul Revere House in Boston. She was senior museum educator at the Smithsonian Early Enrichment Center for nine years where she led professional development seminars for educators and museum professionals in using museum resources with young children. Caspari is coauthor of *Guided Inquiry: Learning in the 21st Century*.